▶ **American Presidential Power and the War on Terror**

DOI: 10.1057/9781137539625.0001

Other Palgrave Pivot titles

Christopher Perkins: The United Red Army on Screen: Cinema, Aesthetics and The Politics of Memory

Susanne Lundin: Organs for Sale: An Ethnographic Examination of the International Organ Trade

Margot Finn and Kate Smith: New Paths to Public Histories

Vicky Duckworth and Gordon Ade-Ojo: Adult Literacy Policy and Practice: From Intrinsic Values to Instrumentalism

Brendan Howe: Democratic Governance in Northeast Asia: A Human-Centred Approach to Evaluating Democracy

Evie Kendal: Equal Opportunity and the Case for State Sponsored Ectogenesis

Joseph Watras: Philosophies of Environmental Education and Democracy: Harris, Dewey, and Bateson on Human Freedoms in Nature

Christos Kourtelis: The Political Economy of Euro-Mediterranean Relations: European Neighbourhood Policy in North Africa

Liz Montegary and Melissa Autumn White (editors): Mobile Desires: The Politics and Erotics of Mobility Justice

Anna Larsson and Sanja Magdalenić: Sociology in Sweden: A History

Philip Whitehead: Reconceptualising the Moral Economy of Criminal Justice: A New Perspective

Robert Kerr: How Postmodernism Explains Football and Football Explains Postmodernism: The Billy Clyde Conundrum

Ilan Bijaoui: The Open Incubator Model: Entrepreneurship, Open Innovation, and Economic Development in the Periphery

Pilar Melero: Mythological Constructs of Mexican Femininity

Rafael Kandiyoti: Powering Europe: Russia, Ukraine, and the Energy Squeeze

Cristina Sánchez-Conejero: Sex and Ethics in Spanish Cinema

Matthew Gritter: The Policy and Politics of Food Stamps and SNAP

Bridget Kevane: The Dynamics of Jewish Latino Relationships: Hope and Caution

Nataly Z. Chesky, Mark R. Wolfmeyer: Philosophy of STEM Education: A Critical Investigation

Seung Ho Park, Gerardo R. Ungson, and Andrew Cosgrove: Scaling the Tail: Managing Profitable Growth in Emerging Markets

DOI: 10.1057/9781137539625.0001

palgrave▸pivot

▶

American Presidential Power and the War on Terror: Does the Constitution Matter?

Justin DePlato

*Assistant Professor of Political Science,
Robert Morris University, USA*

DOI: 10.1057/9781137539625.0001

AMERICAN PRESIDENTIAL POWER AND THE WAR ON TERROR
Copyright © Justin DePlato, 2015.

First published in 2015 by
PALGRAVE MACMILLAN®
in the United States—a division of St. Martin's Press LLC,
175 Fifth Avenue, New York, NY 10010.

Where this book is distributed in the UK, Europe and the rest of the world,
this is by Palgrave Macmillan, a division of Macmillan Publishers Limited,
registered in England, company number 785998, of Houndmills,
Basingstoke, Hampshire RG21 6XS.

Palgrave Macmillan is the global academic imprint of the above companies
and has companies and representatives throughout the world.

Palgrave® and Macmillan® are registered trademarks in the United States,
the United Kingdom, Europe and other countries.

ISBN: 978-1-137-53963-2 EPUB
ISBN: 978-1-137-53962-5 PDF
ISBN: 978-1-137-53961-8 Hardback

Library of Congress Cataloging-in-Publication Data is available from the
Library of Congress.

A catalogue record of the book is available from the British Library.

First edition: 2015

www.palgrave.com/pivot

DOI: 10.1057/9781137539625

▶ *I dedicate this book to my wife, Angela*

DOI: 10.1057/9781137539625.0001

Contents

DOI: 10.1057/9781137539625.0001

Acknowledgments

I thank the anonymous reviewers whose insightful critique made this project much stronger. I thank the support of my colleagues in the scholarship of the Presidency.

We are all trying to educate the populace on the powers and limitations of the Presidency.

▶

DOI: 10.1057/9781137539625.0002

palgrave▶pivot

www.palgrave.com/pivot

Introduction: The Era of a War on Terror

Abstract: *America's War on Terror is continuing since September 11, 2001. President G. W. Bush and his successor President Obama have led the USA into a proverbial quagmire as the nation deploys troops, monies, and strategies to combat the enemies in an ever-changing battlefield. First, the nation waged war against al-Qaeda, now the nation wages war against ISIS (ISIL). The face of terror is ever changing and with it changes the American foreign policy to combat the enemy. In this book, I examine the Presidential prerogative to wage war against the terrorists and discover that the presidents, so far, have disregarded the Constitution as they determine what policy and what power to use when attacking the enemies and in waging the War on Terror. The findings in this book should cause concerns for all serious readers and lovers of American liberty. During this War on Terror, the nation is under the control of presidential decree and orders, rather than deliberative Congressional policy.*

DePlato, Justin. *American Presidential Power and the War on Terror: Does the Constitution Matter?* New York: Palgrave Macmillan, 2015. DOI: 10.1057/9781137539625.0003.

With a foghorn blowing, standing atop the ruble of the World Trade Center, President G. W. Bush declared to the world, "we have heard you, soon you will hear us." With that statement, following the gruesome attacks of September 11, 2001, the USA would begin a "War on Terror." The enemy, not the normal conventional standing army of the yesteryears—but the enemy was and—is an enigmatic decentralized group with no nation, country, or clearly stated boundaries. With the passage of time the enemy has changed, the names have changed, the threats have changed, and the war has changed. What has not changed is the fervent resolve of the West to destroy and dismantle the terrorist groups, mainly Islamic militants.

Since September 11, 2001 the USA and most of the Western allies have been in a perpetual state of emergency. With emergency come emergency laws. In the USA, such emergency laws are the Patriot Act and the hidden power clauses in the National Defense Reauthorization Acts. These extraordinary powers, during crisis, include enhanced interrogations, free-ranging rendition, expansive searches and seizures of private property, the defining of enemy combatants, the use of drones to strike and kill enemy combatants, the seizing of press documents without prior consent, the use of special military bases to detain the enemies, using the Intelligence community to spy on all potential threats via the PRISM program (a massive metadata surveillance program), and the blatant repudiation of laws such as the War Power Resolutions of the 1970s. All of these actions were taken by an American president, in his humble opinion, to protect the American people. Yet, such actions often brazenly defy the law, and are frankly, oftentimes unconstitutional and criminal. In this book, I explore a very important topic that all scholars and modern citizens should take heed of. What are the powers of the Presidency in times of crisis? What limitations exist on President Power in times of crisis? Do presidents have the right to violate the law in time of crisis? Are there any provisions in the Constitution, which grant the president emergency powers? Finally, does the Constitution even matter, or rather can a president do whatever he wants in time of crisis to defeat the enemy with consideration for or against the Constitution?

To answer these questions I analyze and investigate two very important cases of presidents using emergency power, in light of the War on Terror. The presidencies of G. W. Bush and Barack Obama are studied to understand their interpretations of power in light of crisis, and to understand the ramifications, justifications, and consequences of using such extraordinary power, to protect the nation, rather than to harm the constitutional rights of American citizens.

Scholars have long debated this topic of power during crisis. For the sake of simplicity, I divide the literature between twentieth- and twenty-first-century thinkers.

Twentieth-century thinkers

Frederick Watkins, while studying the Weimer experience and crisis government, suggested that emergency powers are constructed to preserve the established institutions from "the danger of permanent injury in a period of temporary emergency."[1] He stated, "the dictatorship serves to protect established institutions from the danger of permanent injury in a period of temporary emergency, and is followed by a prompt return to the previous forms of political life." He suggested, then, "I can see no reason why absolutism should not be used as a means for the defense of liberal institutions."[2]

Furthermore, Watkins outlined two key elements of the problem of emergency governance: (1) increasing administrative powers of the executive, while, (2) simultaneously imposing limitations on that power. He rejected the idea that legislative checks on the exercise of executive emergency powers would be an effective method of imposing limitations because "it is clearly unrealistic to rely on the government controlled majority in the legislature to exercise effective supervision over that same government in its use of emergency powers."[3]

In addition, he suggested that the "delay inherent in judicial proceedings" would limit the court's ability to respond to a crisis appropriately. Therefore, Watkins argued, the dictatorship and broad use of emergency powers should rest with the executive leader. However, he did place conditions and limitations on this leader: (1) "the period of dictatorship must be relatively short," (2) "dictatorship should always be strictly legitimate in character," and (3) "final authority to determine the need for dictatorship in any given case must never rest with the dictator himself."[4] In conclusion, Watkins thoroughly warned that the objective of an emergency executive—or as he termed it, constitutional dictator—should be "strict political conservatism,"[5] staying within the boundaries of the law as the constitution proscribed for creating an emergency dictator.

DOI: 10.1057/9781137539625.0003

Carl Friedrich agreed with Watkins's main points for creating a constitutional dictatorship. He acknowledged that during a period of emergency the difficulty lies in being able to cope with the doctrine of separation of powers (which, although it creates balance in government, also causes delays in governmental processes), at the same time stressing the necessity to deal with the emergency swiftly and appropriately. He suggested that the greatest challenge during the emergency is "to cope with the situations of unprecedented magnitude and gravity." He averred, "there must be a broad grant of powers, subject to equally strong limitations as to who shall exercise such powers, when, for how long, and to what end."[6]

To summarize Friedrich's main points supporting the creation of a constitutional dictator, "(1) the dictator must be derived from constitutional means and, therefore, legitimate; (2) he must not be able to determine his own emergency powers; (3) the emergency powers must be exercised under a strict time limitation; and (4) the objective of emergency action must be the defense of the constitutional order."[7]

Friedrich conceded that there are very few, if any, true institutional safeguards to prevent the constitutional democracy from completely degrading into a dictatorship following or during the emergency. Although it may seem that Friedrich feared a complete devolution of the constitutional state during an emergency, he did offer one solution to prevent out-of-control tyranny: the role of the courts during, and after the crisis. Friedrich stated, "the courts, even though helpless in the face of a real emergency, may play a role to restrict the use of emergency powers to legitimate ends." He went on to state that the courts may "act as a sort of keeper of the President's and the people's conscience."[8]

Probably the most influential contribution on the matter of executive emergency power in modern democracies is of Clinton Rossiter. In his classic *Constitutional Dictatorship*, he explored four distinct case studies, each a nation that faced major crises in the early to mid-twentieth century as a consequence of world wars. His study focuses on Great Britain, France, Germany, and the USA. In each case, he examined the causes in the political system or, rather, the weaknesses that brought forth a constitutional dictatorship. From this examination, he concluded that in modern Western democracies the inherent weakness or flaw in the system is government's structural inabilities to deal with crises without resorting to unusual means.

DOI: 10.1057/9781137539625.0003

Rossiter offered 11 distinct claims associated with the conditions of success for a constitutional dictatorship. To begin, he argued that a government should not initiate a general regime or particular institution of constitutional dictatorship unless, of course, it is absolutely necessary. He conceded that the only reason for executive emergency powers is to preserve the state and its constitutional order. With this claim Rossiter appears to rely on the Lockean and Rousseauean concept of executive emergency power, which states that emergency power ought to be used only in times of great and unprecedented emergency. Most importantly, he indicated that a constitutional dictator should never have the ability to expand his own authority during the time of emergency. Therefore, Rossiter suggested that the decision to institute the dictatorship should never be in the hands of the man or men who would constitute the dictatorship.[9]

With regard to the use of the emergency powers, Rossiter maintained that the powers and all adjustments in the organization of government should be directed in pursuit of constitutional or legal requirements. For Rossiter, the suspension of normal democratic practices, although he grants that this may become necessary, must still be carried out in a way that does not disregard the constitution. In addition, he asserted that no dictatorial institution should be adopted, "no right invaded, no regular procedure altered any more than is absolutely necessary for the conquest of the particular crisis."[10] Therefore, Rossiter argued that the only purpose for expanding executive emergency powers is to ward off the crisis that brought about the rise in executive authority in the first place. The rights of the citizenry should not be disregarded even during an emergency.

Furthermore, according to Rossiter, the term of the dictatorship should be limited: "the measures adopted in the prosecution of a constitutional dictatorship should never be permanent in character or effect."[11] In so doing, he averred that the decision to terminate the constitutional dictatorship, like the decision to institute it, should never be in the hands of the man or men "who constitute the dictator."[12] Unlike Rousseau, who argued that the expanded authority of the executive should be clearly defined and limited, or Locke, who considered the termination of the expanded executive authority to be up to the "heavens," Rossiter did not explore whether a standard length of time would be allotted to the constitutional dictator.[13] It seems more likely that Rossiter would concede that the powers granted during the emergency would be terminated after the crisis had ended, when he stated that "no constitutional dictatorship should extend beyond the termination of the crisis for

DOI: 10.1057/9781137539625.0003

which it was instituted."[14] In so doing, the "termination of the crisis must be followed by as complete a return to as possible to the political and governmental conditions existing prior to the initiation of the constitutional dictatorship."[15]

Moreover, Rossiter also maintained that during a crisis, the citizenry is not powerless; rather, they will have power because the dictatorship should be "carried on by person's representative of every part of the citizenry instead in the defense of the existing constitutional order."[16] Therefore, the will of the people is still explicit even during a period when there are enormous pressures against constitutionalism. In fact, Rossiter clearly stated that "ultimate responsibility should be maintained for every action taken under a constitutional dictatorship."[17] Thus, even though the executive may have unprecedented powers, this does not afford him the right to be irresponsible.

In a departure from Watkins's argument regarding the oversight of expanded executive emergency powers, Rossiter accorded to the legislature greater latitude in the oversight of the executive's exercise of emergency powers. According to him, the legislature should have the final responsibility for declaring when an emergency is over. However, this immediately prompts certain questions: What would happen if the legislature and the executive were of the same party? Would such an occurrence afford the executive more time and latitude during and after the emergency? Conversely, if the government were divided, would the crisis be terminated sooner, or later? Rossiter did not address any of the aforementioned questions, though he did place great faith in the investigative legislative committees to maintain boundaries for executive power during an emergency.

Finally, Rossiter presented a lesser role for the judiciary during and after a crisis, arguing that because the court is a reactionary institution, its role in the political process will be delayed, rendering it an impotent overseer and interpreter of the war powers."[18] Therefore, the Court's ability to be a check on executive emergency power, at least during the crisis, would be limited.

Twenty-first century thinkers

Further contemporary scholars, such as Adler, Ackerman, Cronin, Pfiffner, and Matheson[19] argue that executive emergency power is acceptably needed in a liberal democracy whereby presidents have a broad or extraordinary power, during crisis. They argue, however, that such power is not unbounded, unlimited, or unilateral. Rather, these scholars generate a basic formula, construed from early American writers that presidents may use emergency power in extraordinary times, with the understanding that while doing so, they are constrained by the rule of law and the following metrics:

▸ The use of power is in consultation with Congress.
▸ The power is exercised with restraint and prudence.
▸ The power is used with "explicit" understanding that such actions are extraordinary and subject to congressional and judicial oversight.

Contemporary thinking on the theory of executive emergency power is confined not only to a discussion about whether, constitutionally, an executive should have extraordinary power, rather than Congress, but also is focused on a debate over whether or not executives may use their extraordinary power without any Congressional, of Judicial oversight. Thereby, the main debate in contemporary writing on executive emergency power is, whether or not an executive may act unilaterally, while exercising his power, or is he constrained by other institutions requiring consultation, or physical restraints on his power? The remainder of this book answers the aforementioned question by analyzing empirical data from the history of the American Republic to determine whether presidents do exercise emergency power unilaterally, or are they restraining their power by seeking consultation and oversight from other constitutional institutions.

While I think many of my contemporary scholars make valid contributions to the literature, I think they fail to see a new contribution to the study of the American Presidency, during crisis. In this book, I offer a slight departure from others by arguing that the anti federalist so were in favor of enumerating executive emergency powers in the Federal Constitution is far more prudent and consistent with the customs and traditions of constitutional democracy, rather than the implicit model that is in place. In fact, I argue that if the implicit model is further maintained and used, the American presidency would remain unbridled and cavalier in the pursuit of the War on Terror.

The American model of representative democracy prides itself on being a nation ruled by law, not by men. In America, the key to

DOI: 10.1057/9781137539625.0003

understanding this great Republic is the doctrine that no person is above the law. The law is bound to the people to serve and protect the people. The Constitution not just provides powers to the government, but also prohibits and limits powers to prevent the rise of a tyrannical leader. The American model has a system of checks and balances, and separated branches, which enables and fosters a decentralization of power; however, in times of crisis the opposite seems to happen. The branches become irrelevant, the checks and balances cease, and power is centralized toward the executive. Why is that the case? In order to answer the question as to why in the American system power centralizes toward the executive, I offer a short trip into early American political philosophy (as outlined in chapter 1) and the competing arguments made at the Constitutional Convention over executive power. While the Federalists led by Alexander Hamilton urge for the competent powers, as we see in Article II today, which includes this ambiguous idea of emergency power or implicit model for executive emergency power, the Anti-Federalists led by G. Clinton, Edmund Randolph, and Patrick Henry, urge that any executive, equipped with the Army and competent powers, will soon come to trample the rights and liberties of all Americans.

In time of crisis, should the executive violate the law in order to save it? Imagine that a person's house was on fire and the owner of the house was out of town. The firefighters show up to put out the fire, but the law mandates that they may enter the house only if given permission by the property owner, who is out of town. The neighbors gather, insisting that the firefighters put out the fire, yet the firefighters, bound by the law, cannot enter the house. Meanwhile, the fire begins to threaten the other houses on the street. Should the firefighters violate the law, enter the house, and put out the fire in order to save the other houses on the street?

The answer to the previous question lies in the theory of executive emergency power, of which, the main contributors are John Locke and Alexander Hamilton. Locke urged in chapter 14 of his great Second Treatise on Civil Government, that there must be a prerogative power reserved for the executive to do things which at times, may go beyond the scope of law, in order to preserve the nation. The leader of a Republic has the extraordinary responsibility to protect the nation and to do "whatever is necessary" to fulfill that end. As Lincoln reminds all Americans during the Civil War, "we must save the Union," even if that means we may have to violate the law in order to do so.

DOI: 10.1057/9781137539625.0003

The fact is, the American model of government supports the constitutional interpretation of executive emergency power favoring the Lockean/Hamiltonian idea that executives have unlimited power in times of crisis (including violating the Constitution). Therefore, in times of crisis presidents are above the law. Even though the word emergency does not appear in the Constitution, the idea of executive emergency power does, as an implied power. I show in this short book that there are four clauses in the Constitution that constructively create an implied executive emergency power. They are: The Vesting Clause, the Commander in Chief Clause, the Oath Clause, and the Take Care Clause of the Federal Constitution. They may, and will do things that violate the Constitution, and I dare say, the conscience of our society. They do such extraordinary things, though, to preserve the Union and the remaining laws. For clarification, the American model for determining the exercise, use, and parameters of power during crisis is an unfettered executive prerogative, rather than enumerated powers in the Constitution. Of course, as is explored in this book, American presidents' claim having implied emergency powers.

Furthermore, as is evinced in this book, executive emergency powers are insulated from the usual partisan divide of Washington politics. Both republicans and democrats will favor strong, decisive, and expansive executive powers in times of crisis. Of course, G. W. Bush was a hawkish republican, aggressive and decisive in his pursuit of terror. Barack Obama, as Senator, a dovish antiwar presidential candidate, but as commander in chief very few can tell Barack Obama's policies toward terrorism from G. W. Bush's. Why is that? The answer is simple. The nation is at war, and no American president wants the historical record to include in his legacy that he lost a war; therefore, the presidents who combat terror will be very similar regardless of the party—either will be decisive, aggressive, and likely will violate the law in order to preserve the nation.

In this first six years of President Obama's time in Office he has already ordered and succeeded in the assassination of over 1500 people, the forceful seizure of AP press documents and hardware, and the defense of the PRISM program. Remember, President Obama won the Nobel Peace Prize; yet, his time in Office has not adhered to the boundaries of peace, especially if you are an enemy of the United States, which includes any American citizen or foreigner that plots, or collaborates with the terrorists groups.

DOI: 10.1057/9781137539625.0003

Quite possibly, the scariest law in America, the Patriot Act, is revered as the most important protective law in the history of the nation. Yet, I urge people to read it, especially clauses 214 and 215. In both provisions the Federal Government has the right to pursue an enemy combatant (with of course, the Feds determining who is an enemy combatant), beyond the scope of their original warrant. This is known as the lone wolf provision of the Act whereby, the Feds if they are pursuing an alleged threat by warrant and they stumble on a new path, new people, or groups of alleged terrorists, they do not have to receive a new warrant prior to seizing and searching out the threat. In short, the logic the Feds use in their pursuit of terror, assumes that all Americans are potential threats (see the PRISM program discussion in Chapter 3).

Chapter 1 of this book outlines and provides an analytical review of the Framers' justifications and reasons for, or against executive emergency powers. The Federalists constructed an implicit theory of executive emergency power, which was later reinforced as presidents adopted such an approach. The implicit theory paradigm is supported via expressed clauses in the Constitution. The only explicit emergency provision in the Constitution is reserved for Congress (the right to suspend habeas corpus and declare martial law). The Anti-Federalists, or the crusaders against tyranny, would advocate for explicit executive emergency powers, of those mirroring constitutional dictatorships of Ancient Rome. A separate government would be established during the crisis to govern and combat the crisis.

In Chapter 2, I analyze and examine President G. W. Bush's use of power, in light of the attacks of September 11, 2001. Bush clearly advocates a right to do whatever is necessary to protect the Union from terrorism. The Bush presidency would embark on and embolden the unitary executive theory and expressively reinforce the implicit model of executive emergency powers.

In Chapter 3, I examine President Obama's use of executive emergency power. President Obama, although reluctant to wage a war, continues to promote an implied theory of executive emergency power.

In the year 2015, the main threat is the rise of Sunni militants desiring to build a new caliphate in the Middle East. There organization is much better than their predecessor Al-Qaeda and their tactics very severe. In just a short six months of existence, the group has beheaded two journalists and killed, execution style, over 1,000 soldiers, and their conquest includes western Syria and Northern Iraq. What will be the Federal

DOI: 10.1057/9781137539625.0003

response to this rising threat of horror? What happens if they attack the USA? What will the Feds do to protect the American people? Given the historical examples of executive emergency power, I suggest nothing is off limits. The central question answered in this research determines that the Constitution does not matter in the War on Terror; rather what does matter is the unfettered executive prerogative that determines what actions and parameters of power would be used to combat and defeat the enemies of America. Prerogative is an opinion not bound by law. The Republic is in the hands of executive prerogative, not bound by the supreme law of the land.

Notes

1 Frederick Mundell Watkins, *The Failure of Constitutional Emergency Powers under the German Republic* (Cambridge, MA: Harvard University Press, 1939), 12, 125–35.
2 Ibid., 124–25.
3 Ibid., 12, 125–35.
4 Ibid., 125.
5 Ibid., 126.
6 Carl Friedrich, "The Problem of Constitutional Dictatorship," in *Public Policy: A Yearbook of the Graduate School of Public Administration, Harvard University*, edited by C. J. Friedrich and Edward S. Mason (Cambridge, MA: Harvard University Press, 1940), 338–58.
7 Ibid., 343–47.
8 Carl Friedrich, *Constitutional Government and Democracy: Theory and Practice in Europe and America* (Boston: Ginn & Co, 1950), 573–84.
9 Clinton Rossiter, *Constitutional Dictatorship: Crisis Government in the Modern Democracies* (Princeton, NJ: Princeton University Press, 1948), 554–65.
10 Ibid.
11 Ibid., 285–305.
12 Ibid., 285–90.
13 Ibid., 554–61.
14 Ibid., 78.
15 Ibid., 135.
16 Ibid., 136.
17 Ibid., 247.
18 Ibid., 301.
19 David Gray Adler, Presidential Power and Foreign Affairs in the Bush Administration: The Use and Abuse of Alexander Hamilton. *Presidential*

DOI: 10.1057/9781137539625.0003

Studies Quarterly. Vol. 40, No. 3 (September 2010), pp. 531–44; Scott M. Jr. Matheson *Presidential Constitutionalism in Perilous Times* (Cambridge, MA: Harvard University Press, 2009); James P. Pfiffner *Power Play: The Bush Presidency and the Constitution.* (Washington: Brookings, 2008).

DOI: 10.1057/9781137539625.0003

1

The Founders' Reasons and Justifications for Presidential Emergency Power

Abstract: *The American Founders were very concerned about the power of the American Presidency. As such, they placed several limitations of presidential power via checks and balances. However, certain parts of Article II of the Constitution are very vague leaving open the mysterious question of whether or not presidents have implied powers. Such an example of implied power is presidential emergency power. In this chapter, I examine the Founders' debate over whether or not executives should have an implied emergency power. I find that Hamilton and others agreed that executives should have unbridled, unlimited power in times of crisis; therefore, in America's War on Terror, executive prerogative determines what powers to use and when to use them in order to combat the enemy. According to this view, the President is in no way constrained by the Constitution or Congress as he decides to wage war against the terrorists.*

DePlato, Justin. *American Presidential Power and the War on Terror: Does the Constitution Matter?* New York: Palgrave Macmillan, 2015. DOI: 10.1057/9781137539625.0004.

DOI: 10.1057/9781137539625.0004

Understanding presidential emergency power is rather confusing and, at times, muddled with irrationality and lack of legal precept. In the modern era, there is little to doubt, that scholars, pundits, elected officials, and the masses have become accustomed to expansive executive power in times of crisis. Often because of the wide-ranging scope of executive power during crisis, people tend to place presidential emergency power in the same discussion as presidential war power, whereas the two powers are completely separate from each other. Not all emergencies are wars, and not all wars are emergencies. To help illustrate this point, in this chapter, I will strictly adhere to emergency power as a power that is used to combat defined emergencies at the American national boundaries. Of course, this means that an emergency could be a foreign invasion, an internal insurrection, a terrorist attack, an economic crisis, or a weather catastrophe. Making this important distinction between emergency power and war power is important, because the Framers of the American Constitution understood emergency power to be related only to the aforementioned conditions. Wars of choice are not emergencies and thereby not covered under executive emergency power.

In this chapter, I painstakingly scour the documents at the Constitutional Convention and Founding of the nation, to understand the Framers' reasoning for and against executive emergency power. The first half of this chapter places emphasis on the debate the Framers had over the powers of the executive. Principle point of analysis is rooted in Hamilton's Federalist No. 70, and the Anti-Federalist challenge to executive powers in papers 69 and 70. As the Federalists make the case for a strong, decisive executive, one with competent powers and secrecy to dispatch such powers, the Anti-Federalists make chilling predictions about how American presidents would appear more like monarchs than constitutional presidents, if given such broad powers.

Many scholars remark on the debate over the composition of the executive—whether there should be one executive, or a plurality. Of course, the Federalists won the debate creating a unitary executive, and in this chapter, I explore how the Federalists won that debate. Hamilton's assertions in Federalist No. 70 are worthy, but possibly they are exaggerated and even a case of logical fallacy (whereby presenting an argument on the worst-case scenario). There is no doubt that crisis creates fear and the nation wants resolve and justice following horrific attacks, like September 11, 2001. Does this mean that an executive may do whatever is necessary to "defeat the enemy," even if it means violating the rights of any

DOI: 10.1057/9781137539625.0004

enemy combatant, which may or may not include civilians? Such a question was answered in Federalist No 70 and challenged in Anti-Federalist No. 69, which gives two different ways of looking at the same problem. Maybe we should enable the executive with broad competent powers to combat the enemy, and maybe this includes secrecy, and frankly, vicious means to the end. Or maybe, we should write laws providing power to combat the crisis. In this chapter, I try to elucidate both arguments using primary documents from the Founding of the nation and let the empirics speak for themselves.

In the second half of this chapter I explore the Constitutional question of executive emergency powers, simply put: Are executive emergency powers constitutional? Presidential legal precedence would have everyone in the modern era echoing a resounding yes to that question. In my book the *Cavalier Presidency: Executive Power and Prerogative in Times of Crisis*, I examined the use and justifications for executive emergency power across seven US presidencies, namely G. Washington, Jefferson, Madison, Jackson, Lincoln, Bush, and Obama. In all but one instance, Madison, the executives violated the Constitution in their pursuit of the bad guy. So often we hear in the modern era, well Lincoln did it, or Jefferson did it, so it must be the law of the land when Bush or Obama use expansive executive emergency powers, maybe yes, maybe no. Does it matter if prior executives have done so? Does precedence equal constitutionality?

I would suggest we step back, look at the Constitution, and determine whether executives have broad emergency powers. In order to answer that question I look at the main clauses of the Constitution that construct executive emergency power: The Vesting Clause, The Commander in Chief Clause, the Oath Clause, and the Take Care Clause of the Federal Constitution. Constructing a legal argument is nothing new, and taking all four clauses together presidents, alike, argued that they have whatever means necessary to combat the enemy, in times of crisis. The empirical analysis proffered in this chapter will, if nothing more, make you stop and think whether the President of the United States of America indeed have such broad emergency power.

The American model of government supports the constitutional interpretation of executive emergency power that favors the lockean/Hamiltonian idea that executives have unlimited power in times of crisis (including violating the Constitution). Executive prerogative determines what and how to exercise emergency powers, not enumerated in the

DOI: 10.1057/9781137539625.0004

Constitution. Therefore, in times of crisis presidents are above the law. Even though the word "emergency" does not appear in the Constitution, the idea of executive emergency power does, as an implied power. I show in this short book that there are four Clauses in the Constitution that constructively create an implied executive emergency power. They are: The Vesting Clause, the Commander in Chief Clause, the Oath Clause and the Take Care Clauses of the Federal Constitution.

Over the history of the United States, the people have become prone to accepting the alleged need for a transition from responsible to an authoritarian government in the time of emergency. This has happened primarily because Americans have become accustomed in accepting an interpretation of the Constitution that suggests that the rigid restraints on governmental authority may not apply in time of emergency. As America has become complacent with this understanding, the people have accordingly assigned to the Supreme Court the function of protecting the essentials of constitutionalism and democracy during periods of emergency, and thereafter.

In this chapter I explore the American perspective on executive emergency power. I examine the debate between the Federalists and Anti-Federalists regarding executive emergency powers. In all, the following questions are answered: How did the *Federalists and Anti-Federalists* conceptualize executive emergency powers? How does an executive respond to a crisis? Is it the sole domain of the Executive, or do the other branches also have latitude in the process?

Drawing on their experiences during the tumultuous Revolutionary War and the inherent flaws/failures of the Articles of Confederation, the Framers designed a Constitution that would enable the Federal Government with sufficient authority to respond to any national emergency. While so doing, the Framers were very aware of the possibility of insurrections, invasions, and catastrophes, which encouraged them to structure the Federal Government in a way to respond to such issues. They understood that in some cases, not all, such emergencies could only be met with the use of force by the military, which might even occur within the Continental United States. One of the main deficiencies of the Articles of Confederation was its failure to establish a Federal Government that could repel sudden attacks from within or without the country. As such, James Madison observed prior to the start of the Federal Convention that the main difficulty of the Articles was the "want of Guaranty to the States of their Constitutions and Laws against internal

DOI: 10.1057/9781137539625.0004

violence."[1] In addition, Edmund Randolph argued along the same vein as Madison over his concerns that the previous government and the executive were unable to combat sudden attacks. Randolph stated at the Convention on May 29, 1787, that "the confederation produced no security against foreign invasion; congress not being permitted to prevent a war nor to support it by their own authority...subsequently rendered the government ineffective and impotent against sudden attacks."[2]

The Federalist argument for executive emergency power

To begin, I examine the Federalist perspective on executive emergency powers. This examination is closely associated with writings of Alexander Hamilton, since he offers the most comprehensive explanation of the Federalist's conceptualization of executive emergency powers. In this review I present Hamilton's argument, which suggests that executive emergency powers are implicit in Article II of the Constitution and favors Locke's concept of prerogative. Although the Federalists agree with Locke's principle idea of implicit emergency powers, the "prerogative," the Federalists' incorporation of such power is slightly different than how Locke might have incorporated them. Locke probably would have favored emergency powers to be completely "outside the boundaries of the Constitution,"[3] whereas Hamilton would argue such powers can be implicit within the Constitution. I examine why Hamilton thought emergency powers were necessary to be with the executive, and why he argued for them to be implicit as opposed to explicit powers within the Constitution.

The main points of Hamilton's argument regarding executive emergency powers are drawn from the *Federalist Papers*. Hamilton offers three main reasons why executive emergency powers must rest with the executive: (1) swift and energetic response to the crisis, (2) preservation of the state, and (3) accountability for the actions taken in responding to the crisis.

Hamilton relies on history to remind us why emergency power is critical to the health of the Republic, in part, because emergencies will occur, and the republic must be able to deal with them. Hamilton historically recalls that the nature of emergency is not unique to one nation or another and that America invariably and unequivocally will

DOI: 10.1057/9781137539625.0004

experience such emergencies. "Our own experience has corroborated the lessons taught by the examples of other nations; that emergencies of this sort will sometimes exist in all societies, however constituted; that seditions and insurrections are, unhappily maladies as inseparable from the body politic as tumors and eruptions from the natural body."[4] In the event of such an unhappy malady—insurrection, or emergency— Hamilton consistently concludes that governments must have the power and authority to use the military to defeat the attack.

First, Hamilton suggests emergencies need responses, and not just an ordinary response; they need a "swift" response. The need to respond quickly, according to Hamilton, will require the executive to act and may call into question the "ordinary state of things." He states, "there are certain emergencies of nations in which expedients that in the ordinary state of things ought to be forborne become essential to the public weal"[5].

Furthermore, according to Hamilton, the boundaries or latitudes of the executive acting in time of emergency may not necessarily be determinate or limited. Hamilton states, "and the government, from the possibility of such emergencies, ought ever to have the option of making use of them, because the circumstances which may affect the public safety are not reducible within certain determinate limits."[6] Hamilton suggests that in times of great calamity the government must do what is necessary to protect public safety, even if this means going beyond the scope of law. This is very similar to Locke's claims that the Executive, using its "prerogative," may have to act outside the "scope of the constitution."

Hamilton also suggests that the executive must have the energy needed to respond to a crisis, which the legislature and judiciary would not have in the time of peril. He states, "Energy in the Executive is a leading character in the definition of good government...It is essential to the protection of the community against foreign attacks, it is not less essential to the steady administration of the laws, to the protection of property against irregular and high-handed combinations which sometimes interrupt the ordinary course of justice."[7] Furthermore, he states, "energy in the Executive is key to the security of liberty against the enterprise and assaults of ambitions, of faction, and even of anarchy."[8] These comments lead scholars to suggest that Hamilton argues for a "strong" executive in times of emergency.

According to Hamilton, the energy in the Executive has four key ingredients: (1) unity, (2) duration, (3) adequate provision for its

DOI: 10.1057/9781137539625.0004

support, and (4) competent powers. Hamilton regards unity as the most important stating, "unity is conducive to energy will not be disputed." He states that unity is necessary for taking actions during time of peril that would yield the most beneficial outcome for the Republic, and that it works in four parts: (1) decision, (2) activity, (3) secrecy, and (4) despatch. Without such key ingredients, Hamilton suggests, the Executive would be rendered feeble and ineffective to deal with emergency. Hamilton states, "A feeble Executive implies a feeble execution of the government. A feeble execution is but another phrase for a bad execution; and a government ill executed, whatever may be in theory, must be, in practice, a bad government."[9] Scholars suggest that Hamilton's latter points speaks to his concern about "ineptitude and weakness" during emergencies or perils as not being acceptable for the actions of government.[10]

During some of the state ratification conventions, a few were drawn to the appeal of Hamilton's argument. In particular, James Wilson of Pennsylvania agreed with Hamilton's suggestions of assuring energy in the executive to deal with crises and perils as he sees fit. Randolph stated, "we all know what numerous executives are. The Constitution has placed executive power in the hands of a single magistrate so as to bring strength, vigor, energy and responsibility to the execution of federal law."[11] Governor Randolph of Virginia all concurred with Hamilton and Wilson, stating, "All the enlightened part of mankind agree that the superior dispatch, secrecy, and energy with which one man can act, renders it more politic to vest the power of executing the laws in one man," especially in times of emergency.[12]

Finally, Hamilton suggests that in order to have accountability and a decisive response to emergency the presidency must be singular, not plural. Hamilton's suggestions for a "swift and energetic" response to emergency are why Hamilton is not in favor of plural presidency (discussed later when examining the Anti-Federalist perspective); instead, he strongly favors a singular presidency. Hamilton's argument against a plural and rather unusual presidential concept of a pluralistic leader was built upon three distinct and important claims. First, the president must be unitary in order to effectively lead, execute the laws, and command the army. Secondly, as precursors of the two latter previous points, if the president was a pluralist officer, it would be weakened in decision making, swiftness to response, and would lack the effective strings of accountability. After all, how can you criticize among five different heads of one body? Which head is to blame most of all? Therefore, Hamilton suggests the president must have autonomy, full control over his domain, and in so doing, this would afford the public with a clear path of least resistance in acknowledging dissatisfaction or praise; henceforth a clear path of accountability would be achieved in a singular executive officer.[13]

Hamilton narrows this necessity for the government to respond to the circumstances and the government's limitations furthermore in Federalist No. 23. In so doing he states, "it must be admitted, as a necessary consequence that there can be no limitation of that authority which is to provide for the defense and protection of the community in any matter essential to its efficacy."[14] Possibly the true genius of the *Federalist argument,* in relation to executive emergency powers, was not to attempt to enumerate all of the powers afforded to the executive, both generally and then also during an emergency. In so doing, the *Federalists* afforded the executive the ability to respond to the ever changing nature of the attacks and their frequency, all of which enables the executive the ability to respond swiftly and with energy. Therefore, the *Federalists* assumed that the national government would possess a broad authority to take action to meet any emergency. As Hamilton suggested, "the government is to possess an indefinite power of providing for emergencies as they might arise."[15]

The power Hamilton refers to is the authority to use force to protect the nation. Again, Hamilton states, "it cannot be denied that there may happen cases in which the national government may be necessitated to resort to force."[16] Hamilton historically recalls that the nature of emergency is not unique to one nation or another and that America invariably and unequivocally will experience such emergencies. "Our own experience has corroborated the lessons taught by the examples of other nations; that emergencies of this sort will sometimes exist in all societies, however constituted; that seditions and insurrections are, unhappily maladies as inseparable from the body politic as tumors and eruptions from the natural body."[17] In the event of such an unhappy malady, insurrection, or emergency Hamilton consistently concludes that governments must have the power and authority to use the military to defeat the attack.

Furthermore, Hamilton suggests that the "competent powers" of the presidency may be "inherent" and even "implicit," especially as they relate to "combating emergencies". This leads Hamilton to suggest in Federalist No. 72 that the Executive will be "responsible for the administration of

DOI: 10.1057/9781137539625.0004

government," and the administration of the government falls "peculiarly within the province of the executive department." He goes on to state that the "province of the executive department will include the operations of war," especially in times of peril.[18] He further states, "the execution of the laws and the employment of the common strength, either for this purpose or for the common defense, seem to comprise all the functions of the Executive."[19] This leads Hamilton to conclude in No. 73 that presidents both have the "power to execute the law and to interpret it."[20]

Hamilton, expressly concerned over national security, writes in Federalist No. 74 that emergency will lead to a greater need to centralize power towards the Executive. He states, "Of all the cares or concerns of government, the direction of war most peculiarly demands those qualities which distinguish the exercise of power by a single hand."[21] He later states, "The direction of war implies the direction of common strength."[22] He continues by stating, "and the power of directing and employing the common strength forms a usual and essential part in the definition of executive authority," especially in times of emergency.[23]

Schelling commenting on Hamilton suggested, "a nation state would want to have a communications system in good order, to have complete information, or to be in full command of one's owns actions or of one's own assets...hence the need for the Executive to have secrecy, energy and dispatch in times of emergency."[24] Corwin additionally observed the unique advantages the Executive will have in time of emergency or in foreign affairs, as a consequence of Hamilton's ideas, "the unity of office, its capacity for secrecy and dispatch, and its superior sources of information, to which should be added the fact that it is always on hand and ready for action, whereas the house of Congress are in adjournment much of the time."[25]

In Conclusion, the Federalists, led by Hamilton, Article II of the Constitution implicitly grant executive emergency power. In Chapter 4, I examine exactly which clauses of Article II support Hamilton's ideas as I discuss the Unitary Executive Theory. Hamilton argues the formal powers of the presidency enable the president to act in times of emergency, and to follow his prerogative, in relation to what he does.[26] This may mean he has to act outside the boundaries of the explicit powers granted to the president, but according to the Federalist philosophy regarding emergency powers, the power to act during an emergency would be constitutional.[27] Hamilton and the Federalists advocate for a president who through his formal powers, which were flexible, would be

DOI: 10.1057/9781137539625.0004

able to address any national crisis.[28] Hamilton states, "The circumstances that endanger the safety of nations are infinite...and for this reason no constitutional shackles can wisely be imposed on the power to which the care of it is committed."[29] Therefore, the Federalists argued for implicit executive emergency powers, wisely supporting Lockean notions of prerogative, in times of crisis. This philosophy, however, would not be shared or supported by the Anti-Federalists, because they feared presidents having too much power in time of emergency, which may lead to monarchy or despotism.

The Anti-Federalist perspective on executive emergency power

In this section I outline the Anti-Federalist position in regards to executive emergency powers. First, I outline the main arguments made by classical Anti-Federalists, Clinton, Lee, Henry, and Paine. Second, I lay out the main Aristotelian arguments for explicit emergency powers. Third, I present the primary references to support the Anti-Federalist position for emergency powers being explicit, rather than implicit.

Quite possibly, the most considerable contradiction between the Federalists and Anti-Federalists concerning presidential latitude and power was regarding the structure and nature of the presidency—in other words, how many people would constitute the presidency? The Federalists make it clear that the president is to be singular, for the reasons of national security and response to emergency, but the Anti-Federalists disagree with this claim. The diffusion of presidential power was an important topic at the Constitutional Convention of 1787. The Anti-Federalists led by Edmund Randolph favored a committee style presidency.[30] This committee style presidency would consist of several members from the Congress who together and jointly would constitute the executive. In fact, the committee on detail, which was at the Convention responsible for hashing out the details of the executive branch, would concede in the end that the pluralistic theory of the executive would be useless, ineffective, and would not serve to unify the nation. The plural presidency of the Anti-Federalists would render a weaker president, and therefore would render a weaker executive during emergencies. After all, the American experiment up until the ratification

DOI: 10.1057/9781137539625.0004

of the Constitution was ill fatedly served by the ineffective Articles of Confederation that rendered the executive impotent and useless. Therefore, the debate over executive authority had already swung to support more consolidation into a single, unitary executive.[31]

The Anti-Federalists did not just disagree about the numerical size or value of the American presidency. The plural presidency, for the Anti-Federalists would render a weaker president, and therefore would render a weaker executive during emergencies. Why would the Anti-Federalists disagree with the Federalists on the notion of executive emergency powers? What did they fear most? In order to answer these questions I examine the Anti-Federalist papers and other pertinent Anti-Federalist documents that support a general idea that executive emergency powers could lead to a tyrannical presidency.

Scholars have suggested that the primary Anti-Federalist concern over the Constitution, and importantly over executive emergency power, was that it "smelled" of a "monarchy."[32] As such, in their writings, the Anti-Federalists would often site Montesquieu to remind the Federalists about the importance of separated powers. George Mason expressed clearly the Anti-Federalist concern over an "unchecked" executive, stating, "it will destroy any Balance in the Government, and enable them to accomplish what Usurpations they please upon the Rights and Liberties of the People."[33]

"Cato" reinforces concerns Anti-Federalists had about the Executive turning into a monarchy: "Wherein does this president, invested with his powers and prerogatives, essentially differ from the King of Great Britain?"[34] Additionally, Anti-Federalists claimed that the president's emergency power made the president, "in reality to be a king as much a king as the King of Great Britain, and a King too of the worst kind; an elective King."[35]

Anti-Federalist concern over the broad powers of the Executive, especially during times of emergency, rested mainly in the Commander in Chief clause of Article II. According to scholars, the Anti-Federalists were concerned that the Commander in Chief power would entangle the president with a "standing army" and could cause havoc for the citizenry.[36] "Brutus," a leading Anti-Federalist warned, "the evil to be feared from a standing army in time of peace may lead to military coups…equal, and perhaps greater danger, is to be apprehended from their overturning the constitutional powers of the government, and assuming the power to dictate any form they please."[37] Hence, a major concern of the

DOI: 10.1057/9781137539625.0004

Anti-Federalists is about what an Executive wielding enormous unchecked power would do during an emergency.,

"Tamony" echoed the similar Anti-Federalist concern that the Executive controlling the army could lead to serious usurpations of powers: "the commander of the fleets and armies of America...though not dignified with the magic name of a King, he will posses more supreme power, than Great Britain allows her hereditary monarchs."[38] Furthermore, he states, "the Executive's command of a standing army is unrestrained by law or limitation."[39]

Richard Henry Lee in Anti-Federalist No. 69 elaborates on their position regarding executive authority, in particular during emergencies and broadly over time. Lee suggests that the greatest concern for the development of the executive branch is to prevent "the perpetuation of any portion of power, great or small, in the same man or family."[40] The consequences of emergency might constitute a period of protracted tenure of an executive, or the perpetuation of one executive beyond the merits or means of the Constitution. Therefore, the Anti-Federalists favored a limitation on executive emergency powers and expressed explicitly to enumerate such powers in the Constitution. Lee suggested to limit how long a president may serve and to what extent his powers would be: "the executive may not remain in power as to enable him to take any measures to establish himself."[41] Lee's general concern was shared by earlier political thinkers, such as Rousseau, who adamantly argued for an explicit duration of time in which the executive may have expanded emergency powers. This argument is also similar to Aristotle's and is evidenced in the Roman model.[42]

What provisions did Lee suggest would prevent an undemocratic outcome during emergencies? Lee cites Congress and the Constitution as the means to prevent prolonged or abusive presidencies rising as a consequence of emergency. It is important to note that the Anti-Federalists do not dispute the occurrence of emergency, nor do they dispute the need to act swiftly and with energy in the emergency. Instead, they are arguing for a more diffused and balanced response to the emergency that should be embodied explicitly in the Constitution. Lee states, "There appears to me to be an intended provision [in the Constitution] for supplying the Office of the President, not only for the remaining portion of a term, but also in cases of emergency."[43] Lee argued that such provisions would fall in Article II of the Constitution. The enumerated powers of Article II of the Constitution, as we may construe from Lee's statements, were to

DOI: 10.1057/9781137539625.0004

include emergency power. I suggest it that is Lee's statement for explicit powers that the Anti-Federalists offer as a distinct departure from the Federalists, regarding executive emergency powers. Instead of favoring a "prerogative" power, the Anti-Federalists favored an explicit statement of executive power during emergencies. Whereby, we should consider in the modern era an approach to a constitutional dictatorship.

Lee's concerns regarding executive authority during emergencies are further elaborated by George Clinton in Anti-Federalist No. 67. Clinton first suggests that placing such power in the hands of one magistrate is unwise. He states, "it is obvious to the least intelligent mind to account why great power in the hands of a magistrate may be dangerous to the liberties of a republic."[44] The reason we should be concerned, according to Clinton, is that when too much power is in the hands of a single person he will become "tempted to exercise his power unwisely, and to grow a train of dependents."[45] For George Clinton, the magnitude of ambition and pernicious behavior will exceed during times of emergency and will lead the president to "unwisely lead the troops, control the army, navy, militia and enable an unrestrained power to pardon and to screen from punishment those instigating crimes."[46] I suggest, Clinton warns fervently of the fears of martial law and the consequences thereof. Consider for a moment the rise of a martial state as a consequence of an unparalleled emergency. Would it be acceptable for the president to unilaterally control the army and subject the law to his own fancy? The obvious answer is, no. Anti-Federalists were dubious of even noble leaders who would not infringe upon civil liberties during a time of emergency. To animate this point, Lee so robustly states, "We may have, for the first president, and perhaps, one in a century or two afterwards, a great and good man, governed by superior motives, but generally this is not a likely outcome."[47] The Anti-Federalists were inherently concerned about the true and sincere motives of the president, since emergencies for them would cause the greatest peril and opportunity for the deceitful and insincere motives of the president to show their ugly head. Hence, the Anti-Federalists wanted to do everything they could to restrain executive power, and this included during times of emergency. How would the Anti-Federalists propose to restrain power, while still affording the Republic the ability to combat the crisis? The answer lies in the authority and autonomy of the legislature.

George Clinton and the Anti-Federalists favored a robust legislature, equipped with the ability to manage and defend the Republic during

DOI: 10.1057/9781137539625.0004

any crisis. Clinton argues, "though the president may recommend broad powers during an emergency, or at any point for that matter, the right of power must be construed only by the legislature." Clinton states, "of course the president is the generalissimo of the country, he may and will command the army, but he must not make war without the advice and approval of the legislature."[48]

It seems rather clear from Anti-Federalist papers Nos. 69 and 67 that the Anti-Federalists were in favor of two distinct claims of difference from the Federalists regarding executive emergency powers: (1) Executive emergency powers must be clearly enumerated in the Constitution, and (2) Executive emergency powers must be declared by Congress, akin to declaring war. If either of these conditions were not met, the Anti-Federalists feared, the worst outcome—the rise of a tyrant—was possible in a democracy. This is evidenced by Clinton's warning of how a deceitful and irresponsible ruler, created by poor construction of the Republic, could lead to its very own demise. As Clinton stated, if the Founders were not careful about the construction of the Executive Branch and the construction of emergency powers, "an Angel of Darkness may resemble an Angel of Light."

One of the most ardent Anti-Federalist and devout libertarian of his time was Patrick Henry. Henry presented, during the convention in 1788, the following key arguments against robust, strong president afforded latitude during times of emergencies:

First, Henry argues, "This Constitution is said to have beautiful features, but when I come to examine these features, Sir, they appear to be horridly frightful: Among other deformities, it has an awful squinting; it squints towards monarchy…"[49] An initial reaction one should have to Henry's words is, what and why do the Federalists' points "squint" towards monarchy? The answer for Henry lay in the notions of executive emergency powers and the president's relationship to the army.

Henry clearly connects the president's power and autonomy over the military as a key reason why we should fear the potentiality for a monarchical demise. He states, "Your president may easily become a king;…the army is in his hands, and if he be a man of address, it will be attached to him…"[50] Henry goes on to state that it would be wise to just grant a king, for in so doing, "if we make him a king, we may prescribe the rules by which he shall rule his people and interpose such checks as shall prevent him from infringing them."[51] Therefore, third Henry suggests that any granting of executive emergency power must be

DOI: 10.1057/9781137539625.0004

explicitly stated in the Constitution, hence allowing for strict application of the law and providing for limitations on such broad powers. But we know from the settled debates that resulted in the Constitution, that no such provisions were declared. Seemingly, from Henry's perspective, the appropriate means for expressing executive emergency powers would have appeared like a Roman model favoring Aristotelian norms of explicit constitutional powers.

Fourthly, Henry suggests that as a consequence of enabling a president without explicit powers during an emergency, civil liberties may be jeopardized during the crisis and thereafter. He states, "The President...at the head of his army, can prescribe the terms on which he shall reign master, so far that it will puzzle any American ever to get his neck from under the galling yoke..."[52] Again Henry's statements suggest strong support for limited executive emergency powers and a direct fear that the ability to reset the powers of the presidency following an emergency may not be feasible. He says, "The yoke will forever endure leaving the burden and loss of liberty, an eternal strife for Americans." In fact, Henry poses the following rhetorical questions, "And what have you to oppose this force? What will then become of you and your rights? Will not absolute despotism ensue?"[53]

Henry goes on to continue his concerns over the easiness of an American president, in the mold of a Federalist, of becoming a king. He states, "The President may easily become King...If your American chief be a man of ambition and abilities, how easy is it for him to render himself absolute!" He goes on to state, "at the head of the army the President can prescribe the terms on which he shall reign master and will violate the laws and beat down every opposition," especially in times of emergency.[54]

A final consideration of the Anti-Federalist positions regarding executive emergency powers can be sufficiently gleaned from the words of an ardent Anti-Federalist, Thomas Paine. Paine robustly defends the principles shared by the Anti-Federalist in his main treatise, *Common Sense*. In Paine's words all Americans must be concerned about a monarchical ruler, and must reject the very notion of having one. Paine asks, "...some may ask, where is the King in America?" Paine's answer reminds us of two important things, (1) The law is king, and (2) Executive emergency powers are subject to the law. How is this so? Paine states, "the law reigns above, and doth not make havoc on mankind like the Royal Brute of Britain...let a crown be placed thereon, by which the world may know, that so far as we approve of monarchy, that in America the Law is King."[55] I suggest Paine's words indicate a tacit defense for explicit executive emergency powers. Why else would he so robustly defend the very essence of the law reigning above, if he is to allow or enable the president to have implicit executive emergency powers? In other words, if Paine desires a robust constitution, which is the manifestation of the people's will, then he would be undermining his argument by supporting tacit or implicit executive emergency powers. Therefore, I conclude, as do the Anti-Federalists that the core argument for them regarding executive emergency powers is to create an explicit, sustainable power that would be reconcilable with the law, not extra-legal parameters outside the boundaries of the Constitution.

Constitutional approval for executive emergency power

Where in the Constitution do emergency powers lay? Are executive emergency powers implicit in the Constitution? The Constitution never states the word emergency, yet, we know presidents use emergency powers. The following chapters will explore and evidence Presidents using emergency powers. Before discussing presidential use of emergency powers, it is important to examine where such powers lie in the Constitution. Exploring presidential interpretation of such powers will make more sense based on the critical discussion evidencing the clauses of the Constitution important in understanding where emergency powers are in the Constitution.

Based on the *Federalist* and *Anti-Federalist* comments and debate regarding emergency power (expressed earlier), I argue that executive emergency powers are implicit and constitutional, and I suggest this because of four particular clauses in the Constitution, namely the *Oath*, the *Take Care*, *Commander in Chief*, and the *Vesting* clauses. The *Oath* clause allows the president to defend from encroachments upon executive prerogatives, during a crisis, as well as to protect the constitutional rights of individuals. The *Take Care* clause allows the president to interpret legislation maximizing his executive branch preferences. The *Vesting* clause of Article II affords implicit powers within Article II of the Constitution, most importantly, the executive emergency powers. Finally, the Commander in Chief clause enables the president to command the army and this is very critical in time of emergency.

The vesting clause

How does the vesting clause support or evidence executive emergency powers? In order to answer this question, it is important to look carefully at the clause to evidence how the clause establishes implicit powers. The vesting clause of Article II states, "The executive power shall be vested in a President of the United States of America." On the surface, or just simply reading the clause, one might suggest that the clause is relatively explicit. The language used is clear, and one can construe that a single person shall hold the Office, and shall have the power of the executive branch. However, it is when the clause is compared to its counterparts under other Articles of the Constitution that scholars have noticed a particular difference. A difference that warrants an investigation into why there is a difference.

The vesting clause of Article I states, "All legislative powers 'herein' granted shall be vested in a Congress of the United States…" There lies the difference I mentioned. The vesting clause of Article II does not have the word "herein" present in the vesting clause of Article I. The obvious question is, why is there an explicit word in the vesting clause of Article I to limit the powers of the Congress only to the provisions in Article I and why this similar language is not included in Article II? It would seem the vesting clause of Article II of the Constitution does not limit presidential power to only those powers that are enumerated in the Article, thus creating implicit powers, including emergency powers.

The answer to the question regarding to implicit powers in Article II of the Constitution may be attributed to Locke's concept of prerogative power. Locke suggested in his *Second Treatise on Civil Government* that if the executive and legislative powers lie in "distinct hands," the executive may need the domain of prerogative powers.[56] Locke suggested that during an emergency or a crisis the executive may need unspecified powers to be used at his discretion with the intent of the public's security and safety in mind. The laws that are inadequate to deal with the crisis might temporarily have to "give way to the executive power, viz., that as much as may be, all the members of society are to be preserved" (Locke).[57] Therefore, Locke suggested that a prerogative power of the executive was,

DOI: 10.1057/9781137539625.0004

"the people's permitting their rulers to do several things of their own free choice, where the law was silent, or sometimes, too, against the direct letter of the law, for the public good, and their acquiescing in it when so done."[58]

Furthermore, Locke's notion of a prerogative power rests on five main principles: (1) It must exist when all other laws fail, (2) It must exist only when a law is not in place to deal with the situation, (3) Events may dictate the necessities for a prerogative power, (4) It must be used only for the public good, and (5) The people still always reign over the power and the executive. The president's authority then rests on the notion that an emergency must exit which creates a void in the law, a crisis of constitutional merit, and the people needing protection, security, and defense must yield to the limitations of the president's authority. As Locke would suggest, "this power to act according to discretion, for the public good, without the prescription of the law, and sometimes even against it" (2nd Treatise on Civil Government), is the very essence of the president's authority and establishment for his prerogative power. Important conditions at least suggest limitations on the prerogative power. However, conditionally speaking, it seems clear that Locke's definition and suggestion of a prerogative power grant the president enormous latitude of power and discretion, as long as two things are present at the time he decides to wield it: (1) A crisis or emergency must exist, and (2) Fear is present to mold and shape the public opinion in favor of the president's use of the prerogative power.

The Federalists, as evidenced in *Federalist Papers* Nos. 69 and 70 supported Locke's notion of prerogative powers. Hamilton led this crusade and suggested that a president must be able to repel sudden attacks, and Morris, the chief drafter for the committee of style at the Constitutional convention, the committee in charge of "polishing" the language in the Constitution, was an adherent supporter of a strong unitary executive. Scholars have suggested that Morris intentionally left the clause of Article II not to read similarly to the vesting clause of Article I. Thach suggests, this was done to embolden the presidency. "Morris did his tinkering with full realization of the possibilities, that is, presidents could later claim that the different phrasing of the two branches' vesting clauses implies that there are executive powers beyond those 'herein' granted."[59] Thach concluded, "whether intentional or not, the difference between the two vesting clauses admits an interpretation of executive power which would give the president a field of activity wider than that outlined by the enumerated powers."[60]

DOI: 10.1057/9781137539625.0004

The Oath Clause

The *Oath Clause* of the Constitution is found in Article II, section I, clause 8. It states that the President "will faithfully execute the Office of the President and will preserve, protect, and defend the Constitution of the United States."[61] I suggest that it is in this phrase that the president both protects the prerogatives of his Office (faithfully execute), as well as protects the liberties of the individual. Of course, the prerogatives of the president become more crucial in a time of emergency, hence presidents should be more likely to invoke the Oath Clause as support for their behaviors during an emergency, and cite the "Oath" Clause as legal defense for their prerogative actions. Calabresi confirms this point stating, "it is a duty of the President to preserve, protect and defend his office, which is, of course, a creation of the Constitution itself. The President takes an oath to uphold that Constitution and the public judges him, and ought to judge him, by his vigilance in fulfilling that oath."[62] As a consequence of the president's responsibility to "uphold the Constitution," it is most crucial to do so during a time of emergency, hence, this clause of the Constitution speaks directly to executive emergency powers—where else would the notion of upholding the Constitution be of more crucial and important than during a emergency?

In order to enforce the "Oath" protection, that the president has constitutionally, the Department of Justice (DOJ) has carved out two primary caveats to the president's constitutional obligation to defend and enforce statutes. The reason for the DOJ's caveats is to ensure the greatest latitude of presidential authority in relation to legislation or actions taken against the presidency, and most importantly, against the president's prerogatives. The DOJ states the following caveats: (1) the president is not to defend or enforce those statutes that are clearly "unconstitutional" and (2) the president is not to defend and enforce actions or legislation that encroaches upon the prerogatives of the executive branch.[63] The first caveat "accommodates the conflict between the constitutional mandate that the President execute the laws and his oath to support and to defend the Constitution," while the second caveat "accommodates the occasional conflict between the role of the President as the chief law enforcement officer of the United States and that of the Attorney General as the advocate of the executive branch."[64] The key and most crucial component of the "Oath" Clause, I suggest, is that the president has the lateral authority to "uphold and defend the Constitution." As such, the domains and

DOI: 10.1057/9781137539625.0004

powers constituted in Article II of the Constitution are projected or targeted towards the ultimate outcome of being the "chief law enforcer," that is, the defense of the Constitution (preservation of the Union). Therefore, the "Oath" clause includes executive emergency powers.

The take care clause

The *Take Care Clause* is found in Article II, section III of the United States Constitution. It obligates the president to "take care that the laws are faithfully executed." Further, the president may solicit the opinions of the principal officers of the various executive branch agencies to help him to take care that the laws are faithfully executed. Both components, taken together, have been used to argue for a "unified" interpretation of laws that the president signs. For example, legal scholar Hertz suggests, "The take care clause is backed up by the President's specific and unique oath to 'faithfully execute' his office. The use of the passive voice in the *Take Care Clause* indicates that the President will not necessarily be executing the laws directly, but only overseeing others to ensure their 'faithful' execution." In other words, the president is a unitary executive in charge of the complete oversight of the executive branch. As a consequence to "faithfully execute" the law, this possibly suggests that presidential responsibilities are even greater during an emergency. In an emergency, the law is of utmost concern, therefore a president and his operatives, who the president unitarily controls, are to exert their executive prerogatives, hopefully, in conjunction with the law.

As the Supreme Court has noted, "interpreting a law enacted by Congress to implement the legislative mandate is the very essence of execution of the law."[65] I suggest, at least from the Court's perspective a president's responsible duty is to "take care" of the laws. But this is not just limited to statutory law; this also relates to times of emergency, in which the full faith of the government must be directed towards ending the crisis. As Douglas declared in *Home Building and Association v. Blaisdell*, "There are two Constitutions, a peace time Constitution, and an emergency time Constitution. In the latter, it is the responsibility of government, mostly the executive, to faithfully execute the laws and to defend the Constitution, with the intent of preserving the Union."[66] Therefore, I suggest, emergencies call for "unitary" executives, not

DOI: 10.1057/9781137539625.0004

to simply take care of the law, but to extend any measure necessary to preserve the Constitution.

Commander in Chief Clause

I now turn to the most important clause in Article II regarding executive emergency powers, the Commander in Chief Clause. Why is this clause of the Constitution the most important clause regarding executive emergency? The answer is because in this clause the president can grab power during an emergency to combat the emergency with the use of the armed services. What could be more critical and possibly more powerful than commanding the armed forces? Edwin Corwin called the Commander in Chief Clause, the clause of "uncertainty and of upmost importance,"[67] because Article II has implicit powers, the President is "left to interpret power," and this is most crucial during a time of emergency. For Corwin, events "shape the nature of presidential power"[68] and thus during an emergency, a critical event, commanding the army and inherently controlling the powers of it is very crucial. The question then becomes, does the Constitution confirm that the president has unilateral control over the armed forces, in times of emergency? To understand and answer this question I offer the following critique.

The Commander in Chief clause reads as follows, "The President shall be Commander in Chief of the Army and Navy of the United States, and of the Militia of the several states, when called into the actual service of the United States." During the Constitutional Convention, nothing much was first made of who or what would control the army. In fact, because nothing was mentioned about the control of the army in the Virginia Plan, many of the delegates took for granted that the Congress would be controlling the armed forces. It was the Committee of Detail which actually inserted that the President, as an enumerated power, would command the army.[69] The Committee proposed that the president shall be "commander in chief." But the Committee also recommended that Congress be empowered "to make war; to raise armies; to build and equip fleets; to call forth the aide of the militia, in order to execute the laws of the Union; enforce treaties, suppress insurrections, and repel invasions."[70]

With the two clauses in place, the delegates began to debate the merits of each clause. Particular confusion began on the clauses, as delegates

DOI: 10.1057/9781137539625.0004

were concerned about which branch of government could "make war" and which branch of government could "declare war." Clearly, Congress' power to "make" war included directing the actual conduct of the fighting, but so did the president's power as "commander in chief of the Army and the Navy."[71] Therefore, the obvious question confronting the delegates was, which branch would actually order soldiers and sailors into action and, which branch would tell the soldiers where to go and what to do once they arrived at the battle field? Who has the power and authority to combat and command responses to rebellions and insurrections? In view of Hamilton and Federalist No. 70, the answer was the president. But were there any others, who supported a view that the president, through the Commander in Chief clause, would have the authority to delegate the military during a time of emergency, even without Congressional support? The answer is yes, as Pierce Butler form Delaware came to some very serious conclusions. Butler, doubting that Congress would be able to act "quickly enough" on military matters if an urgent need should arise, urged the convention to vest the power to make war in the president. Butler stated, "who will have all the requisite qualities, and will not make war but when the Nation will support it... it must be the executive"[72]

Furthermore, Madison and Gerry, two ardent Anti-Federalists joined Butler and confirmed that the president must have the authority to combat insurrections. They noted there might be times of emergency in which Congress is not in session and prepared to declare war, yet a response to the action must take place; the president must be able to respond to crisis at any moment. Gerry stated, "The Executive should be able to repel and not commence war."[73] With the support of Madison and Gerry, the motion passed and the clause was adopted.

Summary

Executive emergency power is an inherent power based on interpretations of the Vesting, Oath, Take Care, and Commander in Chief Clauses of Article II of the Constitution. In Chapters 2 and 3, I will examine how individual presidents have supported this interpretation of these clauses.

Table 1.1 summarizes the Federalist and Anti-Federalist arguments for executive emergency powers and the resulting outcome of their propositions.

DOI: 10.1057/9781137539625.0004

TABLE 1.1 *Federalist versus Anti-Federalists on whether to have executive emergency power*

	Main points	Outcome
Federalists	▶ Favored strength, energy, and swiftness for the executive to respond to crises ▶ Law cannot foresee all circumstances that could transpire to cause a crisis; therefore, executive emergency power must be implicit	Centralized power
Anti-Federalists	▶ Distrust for executive power ▶ Diffuse emergency power among the branches ▶ Maintain balanced system of power ▶ Create explicit laws for executive emergency power	Decentralized power

As indicated in Table 1.1, the Federalists favored an implicit model for executive emergency power because they agreed with Lockean principles that because not all emergencies can be foreseen, laws cannot be written for all emergencies; thus, the legislature will be too slow to act swiftly and with energy. Consequently, the Federalists favored a centralization of power during a crisis.

The Anti-Federalists, however, opposed the Federalists' position; instead, the Anti-Federalists took a more Montesquieuean and Machiavellian approach to executive emergency power. Because they believed that the law should be paramount in all situations, including emergencies, they favored explicit laws that granted executive emergency power, thereby creating boundaries and limitations on emergency power. The Anti-Federalists wanted to reduce the risk of an executive becoming a tyrant as a result of gaining too much power; hence, they advocated that power should be decentralized, even during emergency, so as to maintain a balanced system of separation of powers.

Based on the constitutional analysis above, executive emergency power appears to be inherent, or at least implied, in Article II of the Constitution; therefore, the Federalists prevailed. By interpreting the Vesting, Oath, Commander-in-Chief, and Take Care clauses of Article II of the Constitution, we see that executive emergency power is an inherent power. Not only have individual presidents, the action of whom I

DOI: 10.1057/9781137539625.0004

analyze later in this book, demonstrated in practice this interpretation of Article II, but the Supreme Court has also validated the inherent emergency power argument in its *Youngstown Sheet and Tube Co. v. Sawyer* (343 U.S. 579, 1952) ruling (also known as the Steel Seizure Case). In it, in Justice Robert H. Jackson's concurrent opinion, presidential emergency power may exist only under the following conditions:

1 When the President acts pursuant to an express or implied authorization of Congress, the President's authority is at its greatest.

   When the President acts in the absence of either a congressional grant or denial of authority, he can only rely upon his own independent powers, but there is a zone in which he and Congress may have concurrent authority. When this is the case, the test depends on the imperatives of events and contemporary imponderables rather than on abstract theories of law.

2 When the President takes measures incompatible with the expressed or implied will of Congress, the authority of the President is at its lowest.

In the instance of the president seizing the steel mills, the Court found that Congress had explicated that the president may not do so, plus no clear emergency existed, hence the president had no authority to use emergency power, even if they may be implicit within Article II of the Constitution.

Let me pose this question: if the president has the sworn duty to uphold and defend the Constitution—thus, also, presumably the Union—as well as the authority to command the army and the obligation to execute the laws, and Article II does not limit him to powers herein, then should we agree that presidents have inherent emergency power? Or, to put it another way, if the Founders believed that the president should have emergency power, then why not state such power explicitly? Establishing that the executive has emergency power would not limit his power, per se, but it would make clear that he at least does have such authority. Professors Richard Neustadt and Louis Fisher have both argued that because the power is not stated explicitly, it does not exist, and furthermore, before a president can command and use the military, the Congress must first declare war and then instruct a president to proceed.[74] They would suggest even in time of emergency Congress can act quickly enough to grant the president authority to respond to a crisis.[75] In an earlier book I wrote, the "Cavalier Presidency," I make

DOI: 10.1057/9781137539625.0004

the case that modern executives, in their fight against terror, act very cavalier when justifying, deciding, and using their executive power[76]. The examples of power are shocking: extraordinary rendition, enhanced interrogation, seizing private press credentials and computers, expansive domestic surveillance, and limitless warrant access, just to name a few.

In the following chapters, I explore and evidence presidential interpretation of emergency power and show that presidents agree with the Federalist interpretation; the question becomes, why do they act without Congressional consent? Not all will act without congressional consent, but some will, and is the Republic safe in the hands of a president during time of emergency?

Conclusion

In this chapter, I examined the early American support and disagreement over executive emergency power. The Federalists clearly advocated for a decisive, secretive, and competent executive powers that most likely would be used in times of emergency. Hamilton and his cohorts favored the Lockean proscription of an "executive prerogative" in determining what and how to use executive emergency power. The Framers understood executive emergency power as implied in the Constitution, Article II, from various expressed powers. Overall, though, the American model for executive emergency power would become an unfettered executive prerogative to determine and exercise said powers. In the light of this finding, the conclusion may be drawn that accordingly to the Framers the Constitution is rather meaningless during crises and intended to be so. Meanwhile, the Anti-Federalists argued for explicit or enumerated emergency powers. Of course, the power to suspend habeas corpus was reserved to Congress, but nothing else explicitly exists in the Constitution to handle or combat crisis. Thereby, I assert that the Anti-Federalist's would have favored something akin to a constitutional dictator in time of crisis. The War on Terror, of course, an endless and limitless war, poses an outstanding problem for the American Republic. If modern presidents adopt support for the Federalist argument favoring an extraordinarily powerful executive in times of crisis, then what limitations would be placed on an endless war, like the War on Terror? Might presidents do whatever is necessary to win the war? Does that mean violating the Constitution and civil liberties? Did the Founders

DOI: 10.1057/9781137539625.0004

envision an endless war? Perpetuity of crisis should scare all of us, and in so doing, may scare us into submission to an absolute, powerful executive. If the paradigm for emergency power is implied, then ultimately the executive using his prerogative determines what and how to exercise powers to combat the War on Terror. Therefore, there are no limitations on his authority being not bound by the Constitution; rather the power is only bound by his own prerogative. The War on Terror then is fought from the Executive Office, not from Congress, and the power used to fight the war is the executive's prerogative, not enumerated powers in the Constitution. This paradigm then suggests that the Constitution does not matter in time of crisis, and quite possibly means the actions taken during a crisis will be unconstitutional.

Notes

1   Madison, James. *The Papers of James Madison* (Chicago: University of Chicago Press, 1962) 345 and 350.
2   Randolph, Edmund. "Second Day of Convention, Randolph's Note and Speeches," in *The Records of the Federal Convention of 1787,* edited by Farrand (New Haven, CT: Yale University Press, 1911).
3   Locke, John. "Second Treatise on Government," in Classics of Moral and Political Theory, edited by Morgan (Cambridge, New York: Cambridge University Press, 1993).
4   Hamilton, Alexander. *In Federalist Papers* (Penguin Press NY 1925), No. 28.
5   Ibid., No. 36.
6   Ibid., No. 39.
7   Ibid. No. 70.
8   Ibid.
9   Ibid.
10 Ibid.
11 Ibid.
12 Ibid.
13 Ibid.
14 Ibid., No. 23.
15 Ibid., No. 34.
16 Ibid., No. 28.
17 Ibid.
18 Ibid., No. 72.
19 Ibid.
20 Ibid., No. 73.

DOI: 10.1057/9781137539625.0004

21 Ibid., No 74.

22 Ibid.

23 Ibid.

24 Schelling, Thomas. "Hamilton and Emergency Power." *Journal of Strategy and Conflict* 18 (1960): 34–36.

25 Corwin, Edward. *The Office and Powers of the Presidency* (Oxford University Press, Oxford England, 1935).

26 Federalist No. 70.

27 Ibid.

28 Ibid.

29 Ibid.

30 Other Anti-Federalists to support Randolph's position included Patrick Henry, George Clinton, George Mason, and Eldridge Gerry.

31 Even Madison agreed with Hamilton to consolidate executive power into a single person.

32 Corwin, Edward. *The Office and Powers of the Presidency* (Oxford University Press, Oxford England, 1935).

33 Mason, George. *Anti federalist papers* (Penguin Press New York, 1925), No. 68.

34 Drawn from Anti-Federalist Papers.

35 Ibid.

36 Ibid.

37 Ibid.

38 Ibid.

39 Ibid.

40 Lee, *Anti federalist papers* (Penguin Press New York, 1925), No. 69.

41 Ibid.

42 Specifically Rousseau calls for a specific duration of time for emergency power usage and Aristotle's explicit model of emergency power is elaborated in the Roman model used during the Republic era.

43 Ibid.

44 Clinton, *Anti federalist papers* (Penguin Press New York, 1925), No. 67.

45 Ibid.

46 Ibid.

47 Lee, *Anti federalist papers* (Penguin Press New York, 1925), No. 69.

48 Ibid.

49 Ibid.

50 Henry, Patrick. *Give Me Liberty, Or Give Me Death, Archives of US documents*, Random House New York, 1985.

51 Ibid.

52 Ibid.

53 Ibid.

54 Ibid.

DOI: 10.1057/9781137539625.0004

55   Paine, Thomas. *Common Sense*. (Mineola, NY: Dover Thrift Editions, 1997).
56   Locke, John. Supra at chapter 1, sec. chapter XIV, sec. 106 Second Treatise on Civil Government. In Morgan, *Classics of Moral and Political Theory*.
57   Ibid., supra at 22.
58   Ibid.
59   Thach, Charles. *Creating the Presidency* (Oxford Press, 1996) pp. 21–30.
60   Ibid., p. 24.
61   Article II, Section I United States Constitution.
62   Calabresi, Steven. "Advice to the Next Conservative President of the United States." *Harvard Journal of Law and Public Policy*. 24:369. Spring 2001.
63   Stephen Calibrasi, "Executive Discretion and the Congressional Defense of Statutes." *Yale Law Journal*. 92:970. May, 1983, pp. 973.
64   Ibid., pp. 973–74.
65   *Bowsher v. Synar*. 478 U.S. 714 (1986).
66   *Home Building and Association v. Blaisdell* (1934)
67   Corwin, Edward. *The Office and Powers of the Presidency* (Oxford University Press, Oxford England, 1935).
68   Ibid.
69   Corwin, Edward. *The Office and Powers of the Presidency*. Oxford Press: 1945: pp. 15–35.
70   Ibid. at pp. 15–21.
71   Ibid. at p. 23.
72   Butler, Pierce. *Papers from the Constitutional Convention 1787* (Oxford university Press, Oxford, 1925).
73   Gerry, Randolph. *Papers from the Constitutional Convention 1787* (Oxford university Press, Oxford, 1925).
74   See Richard E. Neustadt, *Presidential Power and the Modern Presidents: The Politics of Leadership from Roosevelt to Reagan* (New York: Free Press, 1990); and Louis Fisher, *Presidential War Power* (Lawrence: University Press of Kansas, 2004). Both scholars argue that emergency power is a shared power between Congress and the presidency.
75   Ibid., 92.
76   DePlato, Justin. *The Cavalier Presidency: Executive Power and Prerogative in Times of Crisis* (Lexington Books, 2014).

DOI: 10.1057/9781137539625.0004

2

President G. W. Bush and the Hyper-unitary Approach to Waging the War on Terror

Abstract: *President G. W. Bush faced the worst American attack in the history of the USA. The attacks of September 11, 2001 were clearly a watershed moment in American history. Similar to the barbaric invasion of Rome, led by Hannibal, the USA would never be the same after the infamous day of September 11, 2001. In this chapter, I examine President G. W. Bush's response to the attacks and determine whether he supported an implied theory of executive emergency power. I find through thorough research of classified documents that President Bush did invoke a theory of implied executive emergency power and used his own prerogative to determine what powers to use and when to use such powers in waging America's War on Terror.*

DePlato, Justin. *American Presidential Power and the War on Terror: Does the Constitution Matter?* New York: Palgrave Macmillan, 2015. DOI: 10.1057/9781137539625.0005.

In this chapter I join the scholarly debate over the use of emergency powers during the Bush Presidency—in focus—the War on Terror. Scholars have embarked on scientifically inquiring into the theory of executive emergency power. An overwhelming consensus (Adler 2008, Genovese 2010, Matheson 2010, Cronin 2008, and DePlato 2014) has agreed that the Bush administration overstated its emergency power, and created a new approach to executive power, in the light of the crisis. Of course, I argued in my earlier book that President George W. Bush created what I have coined the "cavalier" presidency. Further, the lack of oversight and shared powers during the war on terror is the hallmark of the Bush administration. The Bush administration endorsed an unfettered executive prerogative to determine and use emergency power and theoretically espoused the implied theory model of emergency powers.

To analyze Bush's interpretation of executive emergency power and his use of such power, following the attacks of September 11, 2001, and the official start of the War on Terror, I adopt a two-throng approach. First, I analyze the administration's odd, but very important, interpretation of the unitary executive theory. The Bush administration will bear a new meaning on unitary executive theory and they will suggest that the President is both judge and jury when it comes to functions of the executive branch. Secondly, I will examine the Office of Legal Counsel's advice to President G. W. Bush following the attacks of September 11, 2001. Lead attorney, John Yoo will offer over-inflated advice, favoring a robust unilateral executive to combat the crisis. Finally, I will examine Bush's signing statements and his actions taken to combat the War on Terror. In sum, this presidency will begin the shift in executive power that will unequivocally result in a more robust, unitary, and extraordinarily powerful executive branch.

In this chapter, I explore the theory of executive emergency power in modern America, following the attacks of September 11, 2001, to determine (1) President George W. Bush's interpretation of emergency power following the attacks, and (2) how Bush's interpretation of executive emergency power either agreed or disagreed philosophically with that of the previous thinkers and presidents. The Bush presidency, in all, will embark into two new American wars; will forever change the face of interrogation; will change rendition laws; will enhance domestic surveillance (PRISM program); will intimidate and strain relations between branches of government; will detain combatants indefinitely in military prisons; will redefine the meaning of "enemy combatant"; and will forever make America live in a perpetual war of all, against all, with no end, but with

DOI: 10.1057/9781137539625.0005

just more and more enemies. The Bush Administration will support, universally, the implied theory approach to emergency power and will defend its position using Hamiltonian arguments. The Bush team clearly endorsed an unfettered executive prerogative in determining what and when to use emergency powers. The Bush administration will not seek Congressional insight, or oversight, in the execution of their strategy to detain and interrogate enemy combatants, during the War on Terror. The Bush Administration will also develop and expound on the intelligence gathering provisions of the Patriot Act and thereby create the PRISM program (a highly developed Meta data collecting program).

To reiterate (for point of clarification and importance), in order to understand President Bush's interpretation of emergency power, I will examine three key areas of thought: The Unitary Executive Theory; the Office of Legal Counsel Opinions following the attacks of September 11, 2001; and Presidential Signing Statements. An understanding of the Unitary Executive Theory is important because President Bush will support the theory, but offer a nuanced interpretation favoring a strong presidency and a vigorous use of all presidential power unconstrained by congressional oversight or consultation.[1] Such an interpretation of presidential authority is similar to that of an imperialist president, and is very critical in times of emergency.

The central questions concerning the Unitary Executive Theory are (1) Is the theory a correct interpretation of Hamilton's words in the *Federalist Papers*, and (2) Does the theory suggest that a president may do whatever he wants in time of an emergency?

Bush sought advice from his Office of Legal Counsel (OLC) for legal justification of emergency power. In the OLC opinions, Bush advisors relied on Hamilton's interpretation of executive emergency power, drawn from the *Federalist Papers*, to define and justify Bush's use of emergency power following the attacks of September 11, 2001.

The unitary executive theory

According to the proponents of the Unitary Executive Theory, the concept is rooted in the writings of Alexander Hamilton, particularly in the *Federalist Papers*.[2] The *Federalist Papers* were composed and distributed shortly after the Constitutional Convention, during which the founders discussed and ultimately drafted the new constitution. The papers were distributed for the purpose of debating central issues of the convention

DOI: 10.1057/9781137539625.0005

concerning the federal government. Hamilton, Madison, and Jay wrote the articles with the hope of persuading readers to support the Constitution.

Federalist No. 70 is the primary source of evidence for the Unitary Executive Theory. In Federalist No. 70, Hamilton addressed the question of how the executive branch of government should be conceived, especially the primary debate at that time: how many people would comprise the executive branch. Should there be one person as president, creating a unitary executive, or should multiple people comprise the executive? Unlike the Anti-Federalist opposition, Hamilton was in favor of a singular, that is, unitary, presidency.

In Federalist No. 70, Hamilton's primary reason for a singular presidency is the need for energy in the executive. Hamilton argued that an executive with energy is "a leading character in the definition of good government." He stated that a single "magistrate is essential to the protection of the community against foreign attacks"; and "it is not less essential to the steady administration of the laws; to the protection of property against those irregular and high-handed combinations which sometimes interrupt the ordinary course of justice; to the security of liberty against the enterprises and assaults of ambition, of faction, and of anarchy."[3] Proponents of the Unitary Executive Theory use this short passage from Federalist No. 70 as a primary source to suggest that Hamilton favored a strong, imperial, and independent executive, especially in times of crisis.[4]

Hamilton claimed that unity is essential for sufficient energy in the executive and "that unity is conducive to energy will not be disputed." Unity in the executive will lead to "decision, activity, secrecy, and dispatch" and these actions "will generally characterize the proceedings of one man in a much more eminent degree than the proceedings of any greater number; and in proportion as the number is increased, these qualities will be diminished."[5]

According to Hamilton, "vesting the power in two or more magistrates of equal dignity and authority" destroys unity in the executive. This loss of unity will harm the executive because "wherever two or more persons are engaged in any common enterprise or pursuit, there is always danger of difference of opinion.... Whenever these happen, they lessen the respectability, weaken the authority, and distract the plans and operation of those whom they divide." Varying opinions may "assail the supreme executive magistracy of a country, consisting of a plurality of persons, they might impede or frustrate the most important measures of the government, in the most critical emergencies of the state."[6]

DOI: 10.1057/9781137539625.0005

In contrast to Hamilton, the Anti-Federalists favored a plural presidency. George Mason of Virginia advocated a plural presidency because he wanted to diffuse presidential power and feared the rise of an American monarchy. This committee-style presidency would consist of at least two men chosen from the Congress from different sections of the country, who would jointly constitute the executive.[7]

At the Constitutional Convention, the committee on detail was responsible for negotiating the details of the executive branch. James Wilson led the committee and conceded that the pluralist executive would be useless, ineffective, and would fail to unify the nation. Wilson suggested that a single authority would be more accountable.[8] After all, who would you impeach if there were several people comprising executive authority?

Hamilton built his argument against a plural presidency based upon three distinct and important claims. In Federalist No. 70, Hamilton argued that "the president must be unitary in order to effectively lead, execute the laws, and command the army." Hamilton suggested that a "plural president" would not be "decisive, would not be swift to respond, and would not be accountable." Dissent and criticism of the presidential office would become problematic; how can you criticize five different heads of one body? Which head is most to blame? Hamilton suggested that a unitary executive would have greater autonomy than would a plural leader.[9] According to Hamilton, greater autonomy in the executive would give the public a clear path for expressing their dissatisfaction with the presidency, resulting in greater accountability in the executive.[10]

A straight-forward reading of Hamilton's argument indicates that he favored a singular presidency, that is, a unitary executive rather than a committee-style executive. The executive would be responsible to execute the laws, command the army, and respond to emergencies. Hamilton did not suggest in any of his writings that the president will be above "any magistrates" or that the presidency would not coordinate with the other branches of government.[11]

However, supporters of the modern Unitary Executive Theory propose a different interpretation of Federalist No. 70 that posits a strong, unitary executive unconstrained by the supervision of other branches of government. In other words, advocates of the Unitary Executive Theory, especially those who would cite it during the Bush presidency in support of his authority, suggest an interpretation of presidential power similar to that of an "imperial presidency."[12]

DOI: 10.1057/9781137539625.0005

The Unitary Executive Theory claims that the executive has the lawful right to completely control and administer the duties of his office. In administering his duties, the president does not require congressional oversight or consultation.[13] This is especially critical in relation to presidents' execution of laws. At times, presidents will object to certain provisions in a law and will not execute a particular provision of the statute, because they claim a constitutional prerogative or discretion to administer the laws as they see fit.[14] Such logic is congruent with a modern interpretation of the Unitary Executive, and will be explored in the following section.

Steven Calabresi and Christopher Yoo have launched an ambitious project exploring the Unitary Executive Theory in American history, both in practice and in rhetoric. They break down the theory into three distinct components: (1) the president's powers to remove subordinate policy-making officials at will; (2) the president's power to direct the manner in which subordinate officials exercise discretionary executive power; and (3) the president's power to veto or nullify such officials' exercises of discretionary executive power.[15]

The first component of the theory, "the president's power to remove subordinate policy making officials at will,"[16] was mostly resolved in 1926 with the Supreme Court decision in *Myers v. U.S.* (272 U.S. 52, 1926). President Andrew Johnson and the Congress struggled over the *Tenure in Office Act* of 1867 that required the president to formally receive approval from the Congress to remove an official of the executive branch. In *Myers v. U.S.* the Court first considered the original debate of the first Congress in 1789, and held that the power to remove appointed officers is vested in the president alone. According to Chief Justice Taft, to deny the president that power would not allow him to "discharge his own constitutional duty of seeing that the laws be faithfully executed."[17]

Dealing with the two remaining components of the theory—the president's power to direct the manner in which subordinate officials exercise discretionary executive power and the president's power to veto or nullify such officials' exercises of discretionary executive power[18]— scholar Michael Herz, along with Calabresi and Yoo, cited the "Take Care" clause of the Constitution as evidence to support the president's legal responsibility to oversee the functioning of the executive branch. Herz argued, "the 'Take Care' clause insures that the president will not only execute the law personally, but also it obligates him to oversee the executive branch agencies to insure that they are faithfully executing the laws." Herz's interpretation of the "Take Care" clause explicitly means

DOI: 10.1057/9781137539625.0005

that the executive agencies are "executing the law according to the president's wishes, as opposed to some independent policy goal."[19]

Justice Elena Kagan reinforced the point that the president has the authority to direct subordinate officials within the executive branch because "when Congress delegates discretionary authority to an agency official, since that official is subordinate of the President, it is so granting discretionary authority (unless otherwise specified) to the President."[20] Here, Kagan suggested that the Congress lacks the ability of oversight once it passes a bill, thus leaving the president to ensure that the law is faithfully executed.

Calabresi and Yoo offered a general schematic outline that suggests that the "rise of the modern presidency," or the imperial presidency, has resulted in more presidents favoring the Unitary Executive Theory.[21] Calabresi and Yoo conceded that, following the Watergate scandal and the insidious Vietnam era, presidents were "reeled" by Congressional oversight.[22] The War Powers Resolutions are a classic example of Congressional oversight.[23]

Following President Jimmy Carter's soft diplomatic approaches and failures in the wake of the Iran hostage crisis and the oil embargos, scholars have suggested a resurrection of the theory.[24] Carter's predecessor Gerald Ford expressed frustration over dealing with an overzealous Congress bent on reducing the presidential authority as a consequence of the Watergate scandal and the Vietnam War. Ford went as far as to state that the presidency was "imperiled."[25]

The Reagan administration is closely associated with the revival of the Unitary Executive Theory. The Reagan administration "created a two-prong strategy of appointing Reagan loyalists and boosting the authority of the Office of Management and Budget to insure the executive branch agency heads made decisions with the president's preferences in mind."[26]

First, Ed Meese, Reagan's attorney general and principal advocate of the Unitary Executive Theory, supervised the hiring process to ensure that Reagan loyalists would comprise the executive branch. Meese stated, "We sought to ensure that all political appointees in the agencies were vetted through the White House personnel process, and to have a series of orientation seminars for all high-ranking officials on the various aspects of the Reagan program...we wanted our appointees to be the President's ambassadors to the agencies, not the other way around."[27] Based on this evidence, the Reagan administration appears to have explicitly intended to recruit, employ, and instruct executive branch officials under the president's wishes and orders.

DOI: 10.1057/9781137539625.0005

The second strategy involved increasing the Office of Management and Budget's (OMB) role in overseeing the administration of policy orders within the executive branch. The OMB acted as a "gatekeeper to insure that the executive branch was following the president's lead and not, for example, being led astray by external forces such as powerful members of Congress or particularized interest groups."[28]

In order to gain greater oversight of administration officials, Reagan created the Task Force on Regulatory Relief, chaired by Vice President George H. W. Bush. Reagan instructed this task force to oversee and review the regulatory process. In addition, he issued Executive Order 12.291[29] to create the Office of Information and Regulatory Affairs that was designed to oversee all regulatory processes within the federal government.[30]

The executive order required "major" rules (defined as those having a projected economic impact in excess of 100 million dollars per year) to be submitted to the OMB's Office of Information and Regulatory Affairs (OIRA) 60 days before the publication of the notice in the Federal Register, and again 30 days before their publication, as a final rule.[31] The second component of the order that dealt with non-major rules (which cost less than 100 million dollars per year), required their submission to the OMB 10 days prior to notice in the Federal Register and 10 days prior to final publication.[32] This empowered the OMB "to stay the publication of notice of proposed rulemaking or the promulgation of a final regulation by requiring that agencies respond to criticisms, and ultimately it may recommend the withdrawal of regulations which cannot be reformulated to meet its objections."[33]

The principle that the president controls the entire executive branch was originally innocuous—based solely on a literal reading of the Article II of the Constitution, but extreme forms of the Unitary Executive Theory have developed. As John Dean stated, "In its most extreme form, unitary executive theory can mean that neither Congress nor the federal courts can tell the President what to do or how to do it, particularly regarding national security matters."[34] Does scholar Dean's interpretation of emergency power mean that the president can do whatever he deems necessary during crisis? In order to answer this question, a review of Hamilton's writings is necessary because it may be possible that modern scholars are exaggerating Hamilton's words in order to favor a more robust interpretation of executive emergency power.

What Hamilton meant by "unity" is plainly not the same as what Yoo and others[35] understood by the "unitary executive." Hamilton wrote that

DOI: 10.1057/9781137539625.0005

the "unity of the executive" was to be understood as the opposite of a "plurality of magistrates": "the faithful exercise of any delegated power" should rest with one man, the president, not only for the purpose of executing power swiftly and decisively, but also so that the public would know exactly who was accountable for "a series of pernicious measures," and that the right man might be punished for such measures.[36]

Furthermore, Hamilton understood the power of the executive as "any delegated power"—that is, the power delegated to the president by the people, through Congress. Hamilton did not think that the "unitary executive" meant unbridled power, since he wrote that the executive might commit "misconduct," which should lead to "punishment."[37] If the president were above the law, his behavior could not possibly be considered "misconduct." In Federalist No. 77, Hamilton wrote that the executive is to be understood as "faithfully executing the laws...of the United States."[38] Hamilton clearly never intended or supported an interpretation of executive power to go beyond the scope of law, or to exist without oversight from the other branches of government. The president has the responsibility to command the army, but commanding the army does not grant the president the power to wage war. Congress must first declare war; the president may command the army into war only after the Congress's declaration.

The office of legal counsel and president George W. Bush's interpretation of executive emergency powers

In this section I analyze President Bush's philosophy of executive emergency powers by examining the OLC and the opinions it drafted following the attacks of September 11, 2001. While Bush did not offer many comments or writings on emergency power, subsequent to leaving office he has often stated that the "lawyers" advised him on his constitutional authority regarding emergency power.[39] Therefore, the OLC memos are significant in determining Bush's interpretation of executive emergency powers.

What advice did the OLC give President Bush following the attacks of September 11, 2001? How did the OLC argue that executive emergency powers were constitutional? Did the advice support the Unitary Executive Theory? Did the OLC provide an appropriate interpretation of executive emergency power? Is the interpretation of Alexander Hamilton's writings correct, or did John Yoo overstate Hamilton's ideas

DOI: 10.1057/9781137539625.0005

to zealously promote a misleading interpretation of the power of the presidency during crisis? To answer these questions I will first review Yoo's argument in an OLC memo dated October 23, 2001. Further, I will review the appropriate sections of the Federalist Papers that Yoo cited and examine them carefully to consider the validity of his argument.

Office of legal counsel

The OLC was created in 1953 with the explicit intent to "maintain the constitutional protections of the President."[40] The OLC provides constitutional legal advice to all the departments within the executive branch and "both written and oral advice in response to requests from the Counsel of the President."[41] Over the course of the twentieth century, the OLC "came to present themselves as agents of the Constitution itself and as guardians of an office whose significance to our nation far outstrips the petty political disputes that consume the daily life of most of those around the president."[42]

Although the OLC has undertaken the primary responsibility of protecting the president from the Congress encroaching upon the constitutional powers of the office, this does not mean that the OLC is the ultimate authority. Political expedience has occasionally overruled the opinion of the OLC.[43] For instance, in the late 1980s, the bill to bail out failed savings and loans institutions reached President Bush's desk first, and the OLC found some constitutional problems regarding the appointment of the director of the Office of Thrift Supervision. The OLC argued that the bill should be vetoed on that defect, alone. Many members of the Congress and the executive branch found the bill to be too politically important to allow a minor constitutional defect to derail it, and consequently overruled the OLC opinion.[44] In other words, the OLC is not the final say on the constitutionality of a piece of legislation, but as evidenced, it is a clear defender of the president's authority and latitudes of constitutional power.

Furthermore, the president shields his office from encroachments upon his prerogatives by relying upon the Oath clause of the Constitution. As noted, the Department of Justice is the primary protector of the president's prerogatives, particularly the OLC. All enrolled bills that go to the president's desk for signature flow through the OLC, "which reviews them for constitutional problems and makes a recommendation to the President whether to sign or to veto."[45]

DOI: 10.1057/9781137539625.0005

The OLC may also play a role in drafting the veto message. If the president chooses to veto a bill, then the OLC may assist in writing the signing statement if constitutional objections need to be made. In addition, if the president is concerned or curious about the latitudes of his power, he may seek legal advice from the OLC to determine the constitutionality of his possible actions in relation to an event, such as the attacks of September 11, 2001.[46]

Office of legal counsel opinions

The following table outlines all of the OLC memos drafted after September 11, 2001 that were pertinent in addressing the Bush administration's executive emergency power philosophy.

TABLE 2.1   *Office of legal counsel opinions, department of justice, drafted following the aftermath of the terrorist attacks of September 11, 2001*

OLC Memo	Author	Date
Authority for Use of Military Force to Combat Terrorist Activities Within the United States of America	John Yoo, deputy assistant attorney general, and Robert Delahunty, special counsel	October 23, 2001
Authority of the President to Suspend Certain Provisions of the ABM (Anti-Ballistic Missiles) Treaty	John Yoo and Roberty Delahunty	November 15, 2001
Applicability of 18 U.S.C 4001(a) to Military Detention of United States Citizens	Unsigned	June 27, 2002
Determination of Enemy Belligerence and Military Detention	Jay Bybee, assistant attorney general	June 8, 2002
The President's Power as Commander in Chief to transfer captured terrorists to the control and custody of foreign nations	Jay Bybee	March 13, 2002
Constitutionality of Amending Foreign Surveillance Act to Change the Purpose Standard Searches	John Yoo	September 25, 2001
Swift Justice Act	Patrick Philbin	April 8, 2002
Status of Certain OLC Opinions Issued in the Aftermath of the Terrorists Attacks of September 11, 2001	Stephen Bradbury, principal deputy assistant attorney general, President Obama's administration	January 15, 2009

DOI: 10.1057/9781137539625.0005

The OLC first drafted an advisory memo regarding the president's authority to use emergency powers following the attacks of September 11, 2001, on October 23, 2001. Assistant Attorney Generals John Yoo and Robert Delahunt authored the memo in response to a request from Vice President Cheney, on behalf of President George W. Bush, concerning how to handle the emerging war on terrorism. The president sought advice on the extent of his emergency power in the wake of the attacks. The president desired to know the extent of his authority to respond to the initial attack, and at that point in time was still concerned about subsequent attacks, even an insurrection or an invasion.[47]

Moreover, the White House needed thorough legal advice on how to respond to the attacks because, according to the OLC, "The situation in which these issues arise is unprecedented in recent American history."[48] The OLC suggested that the attacks of September 11, 2001, were unprecedented because "the attacks took place in rapid succession, aimed at critical American government buildings, on American soil...and caused more than five thousand deaths, and thousands more were injured." President Bush agreed that the actions of September 11, 2001, were exceptional when he addressed a joint session of the Congress on September 20, 2001, stating, "on September 11th, enemies of freedom committed an act of war against our country."[49]

Yoo claimed it was "vital to grasp that attacks on this scale and with these consequences are more akin to war than terrorism...and that the events of September 11, 2001, reach a different scale of destructiveness than earlier terrorist episodes."[50] He stated that "the operatives responsible for the attacks, Al-Qaeda, had a history of attacks aimed at the United States [suicide bombing attack in Yemen on the U.S.S. *Cole* in 2000, the bombings of the United States embassies in Kenya and in Tanzania in 1998, a truck bomb attack on U.S. military housing complexes in Saudi Arabia in 1996, an attempt to destroy the World Trade Center in 1993, and an ambush to kill U.S. servicemen in Somalia in 1993]."[51]

Yoo concluded that this "pattern of terrorist activity of this scale, duration, extent, and intensity...can readily be described as a war."[52] As a consequence of the concerns over terrorist activity the OLC drafted a memo to discuss the president's authority to wage war against the terrorists, to discuss the president's constitutional boundaries in taking military action, and his legal authority to combat the possibility of an additional insurrection or invasion.[53]

DOI: 10.1057/9781137539625.0005

What advice did the OLC give President Bush following the attacks of September 11, 2001? How did the OLC argue that executive emergency powers were constitutional? Did the advice support the Unitary Executive Theory? The following areas of the OLC memos will be outlined and analyzed: (1) The presence of an emergency, and (2) the Text and structure of the Constitution that support the power of the executive to combat emergencies.

Did the OLC provide an appropriate interpretation of executive emergency power? Did John Yoo understand Hamilton correctly or overstate his ideas to zealously promote a misleading interpretation of the power of the presidency during crisis? To answer these questions I will review the appropriate sections of the Federalist Papers that Yoo cited and examine them carefully to address the validity of his argument.

First, Yoo argued that the attacks of September 11, 2001, were actions of "war against the United States of America," an emergency and a clear danger to the civilian population. He distinguished the attacks from that of the previous wars in two ways. Yoo observed that, unlike wars in the past like the Vietnam War and the Gulf War, "this conflict may take part on the soil of the United States," and because the war may be "waged on the home front" distinguishing the "appropriate application of civil law and constitutional law" will be difficult. When the war front is "abroad...there is a clear distinction between the theatre of war and the homeland...making the actions of the military commanders bound only by the laws of war and martial law."[54]

Second, Yoo suggested that the current crisis differed from the previous wars because "the belligerent parties in a war are traditionally nation-states...however, Al-Qaeda is not a nation...and its forces do not bear a distinctive uniform, do not carry arms openly, and do not represent the regular or even irregular military personal of a nation." Because Al-Qaeda is not a "traditional" army, Yoo posited that the "rules of engagement designed for the protection of non-combatant civilian populations come under extreme pressure when an attempt is made to apply them in a conflict with terrorism."[55] He concluded that America is in an "armed conflict with an elusive, clandestine group striking unpredictably at civilian and military targets both inside and outside of the United States." Because Al-Qaeda is not a traditional army and is elusive and very dangerous, Yoo suggested that "the scale of violence involved in this conflict removes it from the sphere of operations designed to

DOI: 10.1057/9781137539625.0005

enforce the criminal laws; legal and constitutional rules regulating law enforcement activity are *not* applicable."[56]

Yoo suggested that the Constitution grants the executive branch power to deal with the crisis of September 11, 2001, and the battle to be waged against Al-Qaeda. Yoo stated, "we [the Office of Legal Counsel] believe that Article II of the Constitution, which vests the President with the power to respond to emergency threats to the national security, directly authorizes use of the Armed Forces in domestic operations against terrorists."[57] He based the argument on the founders' explanation of the federal government's power to respond to an emergency. Yoo also relied on an interpretation of Article II of the Constitution to support executive emergency power.

First, Yoo suggested that the framers were aware of the possibilities of emergencies, invasions, and insurrections, and this led the framers to understand that "some cases such emergencies could only be met by the use of the federal military force."[58] Although Yoo used the word *framers*, he referred only to Alexander Hamilton in the memo, constructing his entire argument solely on Hamilton's remarks. Yoo suggested that the framers (i.e., Hamilton) understood the Constitution to "amply provide the federal government with the authority to respond to such exigencies."[59]

Yoo relied on Hamilton's writings in the *Federalist Papers* to support and develop his argument for a strong response to combat the crisis by any means necessary. Yoo cited Federalist No. 36 to evidence the government's power to combat a crisis: "there are certain emergencies of nations in which expedients that in the ordinary state of things ought to be forborne become essential to the public weal." Yoo continued, citing Hamilton in Federalist No. 23 to argue that the framers afforded the federal government with broad power to combat an emergency: "the circumstances which may affect the public safety are not reducible within certain determinate limits...as a necessary consequence that there can be no limitation of that authority which is to provide for the defense and protection of the community."[60]

Yoo's interpretation of Hamilton's words in Federalist No.23 is a bit concerning because he construed from Hamilton's last point "that there can be no limitation of that authority which is to provide for the defense and protection of the community" to mean that the executive can do whatever he deems necessary during a crisis. However, as I will discuss during an examination of each of the Federalist Papers that Yoo cited,

DOI: 10.1057/9781137539625.0005

Yoo's interpretation of Federalist No. 23 is simply exaggerated. Hamilton was not arguing that an executive can act alone, with indefinite powers to defend the country; instead, as will be discussed shortly, Hamilton was asserting that the branches of government "coextensively" will combat the crisis and do whatever is necessary to combat the crisis.

Yoo cited Federalist No. 34 to claim that the federal government possesses "an indefinite power of providing for emergencies as they might arise." According to Yoo, this power "includes the authority to use force to protect the nation, whether at home, or abroad."[61] Yoo defended his advice that the president may do whatever is necessary within the president's discretion to combat the crisis, with the aid of Hamilton's words from Federalist No. 28: "there may happen cases in which the national government may be necessitated to use force...and insurrections are unhappily, maladies as inseparable from the body politic as tumors and eruptions from the natural body...should such emergencies at any time happen under the national government, there could be no remedy but force."[62]

Yoo argued that, in order to address the concerns of dealing with emergencies, the framers granted that "Article II vests in the President the Chief Executive and Commander-in-Chief Powers. The framers' understanding of the meaning of executive power confirms that by vesting that power in the President, they granted him the broad powers necessary to the proper functioning of the government and to the security of the nation."[63] The distinguishing feature between Article I and Article II's vesting clauses is the lack of the word "herein" In Article II. Yoo suggested that the framers "intentionally" left out the "herein" wording in Article II's vesting clause because they wanted the executive to have more power than what the Article explicitly states.[64]

Yoo concluded that "an executive power, such as the power to use force in response to attacks upon the nation, not specifically detailed in Article II, section II must remain with the President."[65] Hence, Yoo argued that executive emergency power is an un-enumerated power.[66] Yoo cited Hamilton's comment that Article II "ought...to be considered as intended by way of greater caution to specify and regulate the principal articles implied in the definition of Executive power; leaving the rest to flow from the general grant of that power."[67]

Furthermore, Yoo claimed that "such enumerated power [commander in chief] includes the authority to use military force, whether at home or abroad, in response to a direct attack upon the United States. There can

DOI: 10.1057/9781137539625.0005

be little doubt that the decision to deploy military force is executive in nature, and was traditionally regarded as so." Citing Hamilton's argument in Federalist No. 70 that an executive must have energy to respond to a crisis, Yoo agreed with Hamilton in that "using the military to defend the nation requires action and execution, rather than deliberative formulation of rules to govern private conduct."[68] As Hamilton posited, "the direction of war implies the direction of the common strength...and the power of directing and employing the common strength forms a usual and essential part in the definition of the executive authority."[69]

According to Yoo, "Congress has the authority to raise and support an army, Article I, section 8, clauses 12–13, and once Congress has provided the President with armed forces, he has the discretion to deploy them both defensively and offensively to protect the nation's security." Yoo's argument that the president has discretion to use the armed forces, "both defensively and offensively to protect the nation's security," is based on Yoo's interpretation of the "Commander-in-Chief clause" of Article II. Yoo asserted that the president has sole discretion to command the army in time of crisis because the "Commander-in-Chief clause" names the president as the sole commander of the army, and according to Yoo the Congress provides the army to the Commander in Chief who then has the sole responsibility of carrying out the actions to combat the crisis.[70]

Furthermore, Yoo cited Hamilton's words as evidence to support the former's interpretation of the "Commander-in-Chief clause." Yoo claimed that, without a strong federal force, the United States would be "a nation incapacitated by its Constitution to prepare for defense before it was actually invaded...we must receive the blow before we could even prepare for it." Yoo's argument that the framers envisioned the Federal government being capable and prepared to combat a crisis is drawn from Hamilton's remarks in Federalist No. 26 as Hamilton argued for a standing army because "a certain number of troops for guards and garrisons were indispensable; that no precise bounds could be set to the national exigencies; that a power equal to every possible emergency must exist somewhere in the government." According to Yoo, "the power equal to every possible emergency [that] must exist somewhere in the government," is the executive.[71]

Yoo drew from Hamilton's argument to claim that " a fundamental purpose of a standing army and a permanent navy was that they be used in such emergencies...and by creating such forces and placing them under the president's command, Congress is necessarily authorizing

DOI: 10.1057/9781137539625.0005

him to deploy those forces." Yoo understood the president's power as commander-in-chief to "necessarily possess ample direction to decide how to deploy the forces committed to him. He could decide it was safer to preempt an imminent attack rather than to wait for a hostile power to strike first."[72]

Based on Yoo's assessment of Hamilton's argument, this book argues that Yoo overemphasized Hamilton's words and, therefore, overestimated Hamilton's relevance to executive emergency power.

Yoo cited Federalist Nos. 23, 24, 25, and 26 to support his argument that in time of emergency a president may combat the crisis by using the executive powers explicitly and implicitly outlined in Article II of the Constitution. These Federalist Papers do not fully support Yoo's argument, however. Just looking at the titles shows evidence of how Yoo selectively chose passages from unrelated papers to construct an interpretation of Hamilton's words to favor Yoo's argument that the executive is "all powerful" during a crisis. Here are the titles of the papers Yoo used to construct his argument based on Hamilton's remarks: Federalist No. 23 is entitled, "The Necessity of a Government as Energetic as the One Proposed to the Preservation of the Union," and Federalist No. 24 is entitled, "The Powers Necessary to the Common Defense Reconsidered Further." Federalist No. 25 is entitled, "The Powers Necessary to the Common Defense Further Considered (continued)," and Federalist No. 26 is entitled, "Idea of Restraining the Legislative Authority in Regard to the Common Defense Reconsidered."

In Federalist No. 23, Hamilton argued for a standing army: "the Union ought to be invested with full power to levy troops; to build and equip fleets; and to raise the revenues which will be required for the formation and support of an army and navy, in the customary and ordinary modes practiced in other governments." Hamilton claimed that an army is necessary so that the government may respond to crises as needed: "there can be no limitation of that authority which is to provide for the defense and protection of the community, in any matter essential to its efficacy that is, in any matter essential to the *formation, direction,* or *support* of the NATIONAL FORCES."[73] He did not assert that the president may use the army unilaterally to preemptively deal with crisis, as Yoo suggested.

Rather, Hamilton stated that an army is crucial to the longevity and preservation of the Union and that "These powers [emergency powers as the military uses them] ought to exist without limitation, *because it is impossible to foresee or define the extent and variety of national exigencies, or the correspondent extent and variety of the means which may be necessary to satisfy them*, both of which is necessary to preserve the Union."[74] Hamilton was simply stating that a military presence is necessary for the preservation of the Union from potential threats or national emergencies. He did not make clear in Federalist No. 23 that the executive, simply because he commands the army (as Yoo asserted), has expanded authority (unstated constitutional powers) during a crisis.

Yoo incorrectly read Hamilton as suggesting "that there can be no limitation of that authority which is to provide for the defense and protection of the community" and that power rests solely with the executive. Hamilton never made such a proposition in Federalist No. 23. Instead, Hamilton wrote, "This power ought to be *coextensive* with all the possible combinations of such circumstances; and ought to be under the direction of the same councils which are appointed to preside over the common defense."[75] According to the Constitution both Congress and the presidency are responsible for the oversight and administration of war. Hamilton did not explicitly state that a president may use the army without prior consent from the Congress. Such a reading of an inherent power to use the army in time of crisis[76] is possible; but Hamilton never suggested that executive emergency power is absolutely unilateral or that other branches of government may not constrain this power.

In Federalist No. 24 Hamilton argued for a standing army even during peacetime. He warned of potential enemies: "Though a wide ocean separates the United States from Europe, yet there are various considerations that warn us against an excess of confidence or security." He identified the Indian tribes as threats to the nation: "Previous to the Revolution, and ever since the peace, there has been a constant necessity for keeping small garrisons on our Western frontier. No person can doubt that these will continue to be indispensable, if it should only be against the ravages and depredations of the Indians."[77]

In examining Federalist No. 24 this book suggests that Yoo exaggerated the purpose of Federalist No. 24. The primary purpose of Hamilton outlining in this Federalist Paper was to explain the reason why the country needs a standing army. According to Hamilton the need is to protect the nation from external enemies because the nation will never know the time, nor place of a sudden attack. Yoo construed Hamilton's reasons for a standing army to mean that Hamilton favored an aggressive executive in time of emergency; however, nothing in Federalist No. 24 addresses the executive's role in commanding the army, or combating an

DOI: 10.1057/9781137539625.0005

external threat. The paper does not address an interpretation of executive emergency power, only the need for a standing army.

Hamilton continued to argue for a standing army in peacetime in Federalist No. 25, claiming that the United States would be foolish not to have a standing army: "If, to obviate this consequence, it should be resolved to extend the prohibition to the *raising* of armies in time of peace, the United States would then exhibit the most extraordinary spectacle which the world has yet seen, that of a nation incapacitated by its Constitution to prepare for defense, before it was actually invaded."[78]

Yoo cited Federalist No. 25 to suggest that the framers favored an executive able to combat an insurrection and that the Constitution grants him such power.[79] However, Hamilton never referred to the executive in the paper; but only in the government. In fact, Hamilton's statement, "We must receive the blow, before we could even prepare to return it," simply supports an inherent power to combat emergency. Yoo, however, cited this line most frequently to support his argument that an executive may combat an insurrection or invasion without cooperation or consent from the Congress. Federalist No. 25 never asserts that an inherent power to combat emergency is the executive's providence alone. Rather, Hamilton suggested that such power may rest with all rulers, "because we are afraid that *rulers*, created by our choice, dependent on our will, might endanger that liberty, by an abuse of the means necessary to its preservation."[80] Again, Hamilton's remarks seem to suggest he had a grave concern over the power of the executive, as it related to the military; hence he supported a shared venture between the executive and the legislature when using the military.

In Federalist No. 26 Hamilton argued that the legislature will have the power to raise and support a military: "The legislature of the United States will be *obliged*, by this provision, once at least in every two years, to deliberate upon the propriety of keeping a military force on foot; to come to a new resolution on the point; and to declare their sense of the matter, by a formal vote in the face of their constituents."[81] He even went on to state that the legislature is not at "*liberty* to vest in the executive department permanent funds for the support of an army, if they were even incautious enough to be willing to repose in it so improper a confidence." Hamilton apparently supported a coordinated venture between the executive and legislature on matters pertaining to the military. He went on to state that any "subversion of liberty" that may arise due to the size of a standing army may occur "not merely as a temporary combination between the

DOI: 10.1057/9781137539625.0005

legislature and executive, but a continued conspiracy for a series of time."[82] Hamilton appeared to assert that the use of an army over time should be a grave concern to Congress, because with a prolonged use of the military the chances of subverting liberty will increase. Yoo seemed to read Federalist No. 26 as evidence of Hamilton urging an executive to deal solely with crisis and ignores Hamilton's specific comments showing Hamilton's support for sharing the power of the military between the executive and the Congress. I wish to convey here that Hamilton did consistently speak on the shared venture between the Congress and the executive when using the military.

Yoo's interpretation of Hamilton is peculiar. I think Yoo drew broad conclusions from Hamilton's remarks to support his theory of executive emergency power. Did Hamilton advocate emergency power as an inherent power? Possibly, but Hamilton's writings do not support such a reading beyond doubt. Hamilton's only writing in the Federalist Paper that shows evidence of him supporting executive emergency power as an inherent power is availed in Federalist No. 70. In this Federalist Paper one may infer from Hamilton's words that he would assert that emergency power may rest with the executive because the executive will be sufficiently strong, decisive, and, as a singular entity, energetic to respond to the emergency swiftly. Hamilton's energetic executive theory was used early in the republic as Washington combated the Whiskey Rebellion; however, Yoo never cited the rebellion or Federalist No. 70 to support his argument.

I would agree with Yoo that Hamilton made the case that an executive should have emergency power, but I would suggest that the evidence to discern Hamilton's theory for executive emergency power is in Federalist No. 70 and the advice Hamilton gave Washington during the Whiskey Rebellion. In both pieces Hamilton did argue for a swift, energetic response to the crisis and asserted that the executive may act boldly and singularly to the crisis because the power to do so is inherent in Article II of the Constitution.

Furthermore, in an OLC memo dated October 6, 2008, Stephen Bradbury issued a reversal of opinion against Yoo's interpretation of emergency power as stated in the October 23, 2001, memo: "The October 23, 2001 memo should not be treated as authoritative for any purpose...the context of the memo was the product of extraordinary, indeed we hope, a unique period in the history of the Nation...the memo did not address specific and concrete policy proposals; rather it addressed in general terms and broad contours of hypothetical scenarios involving possible domestic military contingencies."[83]

Bradbury concluded that "the October 23, 2001 memo represented a departure from the preferred practice of the OLC to render formal opinions only with respect to specific and concrete policy proposals, not to undertake a general survey of a broad area of the law or to address general or amorphous hypothetical scenarios that implicate difficult questions of law."[84] Bradbury's comments, which suggest that Yoo has broadly interpreted emergency power, support this book's argument. Bradbury clearly scolded Yoo for using the OLC in a way that created hypotheticals and undertook broad theories of law that goes against the intent and purpose of the OLC. Furthermore, and most important, Bradbury made clear in the October 6, 2008, memo that Yoo was creating theories not expressly based on law or related to "concrete policy proposals." Bradbury's comment reinforces my concern over Yoo's interpretation of executive emergency power that was exaggerating Hamilton's words and arguments throughout specified Federalist Papers.

In the October 23, 2001, memo, Yoo reasoned that the president has broadened authority due to an emergency. Based on the declassified OLC memos produced following the attacks of September 11, 2001, the following actions were advised to be constitutional in order to respond to the crisis of the war against Al-Qaeda: military tribunals, suspending habeas corpus for enemy combatants, extraordinary rendition, warrantless surveillance of citizens' homes, abrogation of the Geneva Conventions, unilateral dispensation from treaties, and interrogation methods.

A memo from the OLC, dated November 6, 2001, advised the president that he may use military commissions to try enemy combatants (terrorists). The OLC concluded that the president has such authority because of "his inherent powers as Commander in Chief, the President may establish military commissions to try and punish terrorists apprehended as part of the investigation into, or the military and intelligence operations in response to, the September 11-attacks."[85] The OLC stated that "The Uniform Code of Military Justice (UCMJ) expressly addresses the use of military commissions in article 21. 10 U.S.C. § 821, supported the president's authority to detain and try enemy combatants in military tribunals."[86]

Regarding the detainment, arrest of enemy combatants, abrogation of Geneva Convention treaties, and extraordinary rendition, the OLC in a memo drafted on March 13, 2002 advised that the president "has

DOI: 10.1057/9781137539625.0005

full discretion to transfer Al-Qaeda and Taliban prisoners captured overseas and detained outside of the United States to third countries."[87] The memo went on to state that the president is not restrained by the "Geneva Convention Relative to the Treatment of Prisoners of War," because "the President has determined that the Al-Qaeda detainees are not legally entitled prisoner of war status within the meaning of the Conventions."[88] The OLC concluded that as part of the "President's power as Commander-in-Chief he may dispose of the liberty of prisoners captured during military engagements...treaties regarding the transfer or detainment of enemy combatants do not restrict the president's commander-in-chief power...the president since the founding of the country has had an unfettered control over the disposition of enemy soldiers captured during a time of war."[89]

In a memo dated August 1, 2002, the OLC advised that "certain interrogation methods" are not prohibited by section 2340A of Title 18. The memo advised the CIA to continue interrogation because the Al-Qaeda operative "is withholding information regarding terrorist attacks in the United States and information regarding plans to conduct attacks within the United States."[90]

In a memo dated September 25, 2001, the OLC advised that "amending the Foreign Surveillance Act to include the collection of foreign information as a purpose of the search would not violate the 4th Amendment warrant requirements...the amendment would simply allow the department to apply FISA warrants up to the limit permitted by the Constitution."[91]

The OLC advice partly comprised a response to the potential threat of continued terrorist attacks on the country. Fortunately, such attacks did not occur. Therefore, the armed forces were never deployed domestically, and the suspension of *Posse Comitatus* did not occur. In the light of the OLC advice, what actions did President George W. Bush deploy to combat the emergency? In this section I review the use of executive emergency power following the attacks of September 11, 2001.

I will explore the actions that President Bush took following the September 11 attacks, which exhibited his use and interpretation of executive emergency power. The nation was in a shock after the attacks. News agencies began nonstop coverage of the horrific event as it unfolded. Early reports assumed that the plane crashes were a major accident, only to learn shortly thereafter that the event was actually terrorism—coordinated hatred against the United States.

DOI: 10.1057/9781137539625.0005

War power is possibly the most immediate and obvious example of executive emergency power. Following the attacks of September 11, 2001, many Americans wanted some sort of retribution against the terrorists responsible for the violence.[92] President Bush had to act in response to these demands. Like presidents before him, Bush claimed the authority to use force to defend the nation's security.[93] In the wake of the September 11, 2001, attacks, President Bush sought and received an Authorization to Use Military Force (AUMF) from the Congress on September 18, 2001.[94] Scholars have suggested the AUMF was "sweeping," perhaps the "broadest" grant of war power by the Congress since World War II.[95] The AUMF formally authorized the president "to use all necessary and appropriate force against those nations, organizations, or persons he determines planned, authorized, committed, or aided the terrorist attack."[96] Therefore, the AUMF constitutes the statutory permission for President Bush to launch war in Afghanistan, where the administration deemed Al-Qaeda was located. The administration relied on legal advice from OLC and from the Congressional statute to assert that it would "deal with terrorism wherever it is being harbored."[97]

In addition, the AUMF recognized that the "President has the authority under the Constitution to take action to deter and prevent acts of international terrorism against the United States."[98] As a consequence of the legislation, some scholars suggest the power granted was "unlimited as to time and to geography."[99]

This book suggests that Bush espoused three distinct applications of executive emergency powers: (1) military campaign in Afghanistan, (2) interning enemy combatants, and (3) broadening the military use of Rendition against enemy combatants.

Afghanistan war

At Camp David on September 16, 2001, President George W. Bush used the phrase "war on terror" for the first time: "This crusade—this war on terrorism—is going to take a while.... And the American people must be patient. I'm going to be patient. But I can assure the American people I am determined."[100] On September 20, 2001, Bush launched the war on terror during a televised address to a joint session of the Congress, stating, "Our 'war on terror' begins with al Qaeda, but it does not end there. It will not end until every terrorist group of global reach has been found, stopped and defeated."[101]

DOI: 10.1057/9781137539625.0005

As Bush announced a war on terror to the public, his operatives began pursuing authorizations from Congress to combat the enemies. Some scholars suggest that Bush's ability to obtain authorizations easily from Congress was due to Congress's "acquiescent" nature.[102] Bush's argument that the United States of America was in a "constant and under continuing threats from the enemies" and that "the war the nation faced was unprecedented and of uncertain duration,"[103] aided him in his pursuit of authorizations.

On September 18, 2001, Congress passed a joint resolution without any substantive input into the drafting of the legislation. The resolution, known as the Authorization for Use of Military Force (hereafter AUMF), Public Law 107–40, was drafted by the White House and granted Bush the broadest authority to combat any nation, organization, or person "determined to have been involved in the 9/11 terrorist attacks against the United States."[104] Section 2(a) of the AUMF stated, "In general, that the President is authorized to use all necessary and appropriate force against those nations, organizations, or persons he determines planned, authorized, committed or aided the terrorist attacks that occurred on September 11, 2001 or harbored such organizations or persons, in order to prevent any future acts of international terrorism against the United States by such nations, organizations, or persons."[105] Scholars agree that the AUMF granted unprecedented authority to the president.[106] In particular, David Currie suggested that the president was granted "all necessary and appropriate force against nations harboring or aiding terrorists" and that "the president may use force in order to prevent any future acts of international terrorism."[107] Armed with the AUMF, President Bush initiated what later would be known as the Bush Doctrine that appealed for a worldwide pursuit of terrorism aimed at the United States. President Bush sought from Congress the authority to invade Afghanistan.

Operation enduring freedom

On September 20, 2001, George W. Bush delivered an ultimatum to the Taliban government of Afghanistan to turn over Osama bin Laden and the al-Qaeda leaders operating in the country, or face attack otherwise.[108] The Taliban demanded evidence of bin Laden's link to the September 11 attacks and, if such evidence warranted a trial, they offered to try him in an Islamic court.[109] The United States refused to provide any evidence.

Subsequently, in October 2001 United States forces (with United Kingdom and coalition allies) invaded Afghanistan to topple the Taliban

DOI: 10.1057/9781137539625.0005

regime. The official invasion began on October 7, 2001, with air strike campaigns from British and American forces.

Waging war in Afghanistan had been of a lower priority than that of the war in Iraq for the US government. Admiral Mike Mullen, staff chairman of the Joint Chiefs of Staff, said that while the situation in Afghanistan was "precarious and urgent, the additional 10,000 troops needed there would be unavailable 'in any significant manner' without withdrawals from Iraq." Mullen stated that "my priorities... given to me by the commander in chief are: Focus on Iraq first. It's been that way for some time. Focus on Afghanistan second."[110]

Patriot Act

The Patriot Act is another example of Bush's use of emergency power. Led by Attorney General Ashcroft (MO) and Deputy Attorney General Dinh, the Bush administration pursued legislation from the Congress to empower the federal government in responding to potential threats within the homeland. The government sought a measure to protect citizens from potential terrorist attacks. The 2001 Patriot Act was a 342-page legislation drafted by the White House and pushed through Congress without any formal drafts from the Congressional leadership.[111] There were no hearings on the legislation in the House of Representatives and went through about only one legislative day of debate in the Senate before it was passed.[112] In typical Washington legislative fashion, the bill was submitted the morning of the vote, replaying a common scenario in which possibly many members of Congress never read the entirety of the bill before voting.

The Patriot Act (Public Law 107–56) gave the executive branch extensive and secret power, especially the administration's intelligence-gathering agencies—the Federal Bureau of Investigation (FBI), the National Security Administration (NSA), the Central Intelligence Agency (CIA), and the Defense Intelligence Agency (DIA) —to fight terrorists worldwide. Some scholars suggest that the Patriot Act's broad powers of gathering foreign information made the agencies "too powerful" and endowed them with "unchecked powers."[113]

This act clearly follows the precedent of earlier legislation, the Foreign Intelligence Surveillance Act (FISA) of 1978 (Public Law 95–511). FISA originally authorized federal agencies to gather intelligence on foreign entities or persons suspected of criminal activities with the Soviet Union or conspiring against the United States. FISA authorized federal agents to pursue "the collection of foreign intelligence in furtherance of U.S.

DOI: 10.1057/9781137539625.0005

counterintelligence."[114] FISA made it clear that authorities had to acquire a warrant before wire-tapping a suspected perpetrator. However, under the Patriot Act, Bush officials secured provisions enabling the federal agents to act without warrants in the pursuit of terrorist counterintelligence.[115]

Title II of the Act, "Enhanced Surveillance Procedures," grants the executive another emergency power. It authorizes federal agencies to intercept wire, oral, and electronic communications relating to terrorism or computer fraud and abuse. Scholars suggest that this provision allows law enforcement and counterintelligence agencies to share "information and to conduct sneak-and-peek searches."[116]

Within days of the September 11, 2001, attacks, FBI and Immigration and Naturalization Service (INS) agents began a secret roundup and "unprecedented" detention of thousands of people across the United States. The people who garnered the interest of the FBI and INS were "mostly of Muslim or bearing Arabic names."[117] According to Kate Martin, contributing scholar from the Center for National Security Studies, the "gathering of individuals was a perpetrated effort by the government to arrest people in secret. We have 200 years of law and tradition saying that arrests are public.... We do not have secret arrests."[118]

Critics have observed that, following the passage of the Patriot Act, a "domestic reign of terror visited the US immigrant community because the Act authorized the INS to detain immigrants without charge for up to seven days. But as a belated report by the Justice Department's inspector general revealed, many captives were in fact held illegally without charge for as long as eight months, denied access to attorneys, and then, after secret hearings, deported."[119]

According to a Department of Justice's own report by the Office of the Inspector General, released in June 2003, only one person was ultimately convicted of "supporting" terrorism out of the thousands of immigrants detained. The report criticized the Department of Justice and the INS for using "the Patriot Act and federal immigration statutes to detain, in the federal detention center in New York City more than 1,100 aliens for months without their families knowing where they were and what crimes they may have committed.... It was not until the second half of 2002 that the detainees were investigated and released."[120]

Extraordinary rendition

Following the attacks of September 11, 2001, rendition, or the outsourcing of high-value detainees to third party states, such as Egypt or Syria, that

DOI: 10.1057/9781137539625.0005

use torture for "aggressive interrogation," occurred regularly.[121] Formally, "rendition transfers individuals from one country to another, by means that bypass all judicial and administrative due process...in order to have these high level valued detainees questioned by the intelligence and military communities of the receiving nation."[122]

Egypt, Syria, Thailand, Morocco, Saudi Arabia, South Africa, Jordan, and Pakistan receive detainees from the Central Intelligence Agency for questioning. These nations, among others, use torture as one of the mechanisms to gather intelligence information.[123] After the attacks of September 11, 2001, the CIA secretly began sending high-valued detainees to their home nations for further questioning, that is, according to some, for "torture-heavy" interrogations.[124]

PRISM Program—surveillance of American citizens

In Executive Order 13618, President Obama declared that the United States government may spy on Americans through the National Security Agency "PRISM" program. The PRISM program collects metadata on all Americans, provided by warrant, from all major telecommunication, and social media networks, in the United States. The program intends not to violate the privacy of a law-abiding citizen, but sweeps data on all law-abiding citizens; henceforth, all Americans under this program are potential suspects in the war on terror. Of course, during the Bush years the administration denied the existence of such a program, thereby lying to the American people and disobeying the Constitution.

President George W. Bush's signing statements

The signing statement provides additional evidence of President Bush's support for the Unitary Executive Theory and his theory of executive emergency power. A signing statement is the president's acknowledgment of supporting or disagreeing with all or parts of a piece of Congressional legislation that although the president may disagree in part, he or she still signs the bill into law. Furthermore, presidential signing statements are official pronouncements issued by the president contemporaneously with signing a bill into a law. These pronouncements have been used to forward the president's interpretation of the statutory language. In the presidential signing statement, a president may assert constitutional objections to the provisions contained therein, and concordantly,

DOI: 10.1057/9781137539625.0005

to announce that the provisions of the law will be administered in a manner that concurs with the administration's conception of presidential prerogatives.[125]

While the history of presidential issuance of signing statements dates to the early nineteenth century, the practice has become a source of significant controversy in the modern era as presidents have increasingly asserted constitutional objections to congressional enactments in the statements.[126] Presidents also provide evidence of their particular philosophies toward executive power in their use of signing statements.

To assess whether President Bush supported the Unitary Executive Theory and to evidence his interpretation of executive emergency powers, I examine the signing statements issued during his presidency. The signing statements might shed light on President Bush's interpretation of his executive power during a crisis and may evidence his support for the Unitary Executive Theory. If so, then I can examine his use of presidential prerogative following the attacks of September 11, 2001. Later I will explore in greater detail the president's use of emergency powers.

Like his predecessors, President George W. Bush has employed the signing statement to voice constitutional objections to and concerns with congressional enactments, and, more importantly, to enunciate a particular interpretation of an ambiguous enactment. While the nature and scope of the objections raised during the Bush presidency are similar to that of the prior administrations, they differ in the sheer number of constitutional challenges contained in the signing statements that reflect a strong executive prerogative in relation to the Congress and to the judiciary.

The quantity of presidential signing statements has strayed approximately by 50 percent during the Bush presidency versus that in the previous administrations. President Bush issued 152 signing statements, compared to 382 during the Clinton administration. However, the qualitative difference in Bush's approach becomes apparent upon consideration of the number of individual challenges or objections to statutory provisions contained in the statements.[127] Of President Bush's 152 signing statements, 118 (78%) contain a particular type of constitutional challenge or objection, compared to only 70 (18%) during the Clinton administration.[128]

Which of President Bush's signing statements corroborates his support for a unitary executive and illuminate his interpretation of emergency power? According to scholars Charles Savage, Garry Wills, and a study conducted by the Congressional Research Service, of his 152 signing statements, Bush "cited the unitary executive theory eighty-two times to explain reasons for rejecting some aspect of a bill…he rejected aspects of a bill based on his role as Commander in Chief, thirty seven times."[129]

The following examples from the 152 signing statements clearly indicate the president's support for the Unitary Executive Theory and his interpretation of emergency power. In the signing statement accompanying the US Patriot Improvement and Reauthorization Act of 2005, President Bush declared that the provisions requiring the executive branch to submit reports and audits to the Congress would be constructed "in a manner consistent with the President's constitutional authority to supervise the unitary executive branch and to withhold information which, if disclosed, could impair foreign relations, national security, the deliberative processes of the Executive, or the performance of the Executive's constitutional duties."[130] He demonstrated an interpretation of his emergency power, stating that "Congress is limited in intervening with the President's handling of 'national security' matters." The national security matter in 2001 was the "war on terror," a significant national emergency, according to President Bush.[131]

Similarly, in the signing statement accompanying the law that contained the McCain Amendment (as part of the Detainee Treatment Act), prohibiting the use of torture, or cruel, inhuman, or degrading treatment of prisoners, the president declared that the executive branch would construe that provision "in a manner consistent with the constitutional authority of the President to supervise the unitary executive branch and as Commander-In-Chief…[in order to protect] the American people from further terrorist attacks."[132]

Recent scholars also acknowledge that Bush's signing statements provide evidence of his interpretation of executive emergency power.[133] Scholars have organized Bush's constitutional objections into several categories. Most importantly, they suggest that the objections assert presidential authority to supervise the "unitary executive branch" and to assert command over the army as it relates to emergency.[134] Scholars go on to state that the Bush administration was "particularly prolific in issuing signing statements that object to provisions that it claims infringe on the President's power over foreign affairs, provisions that require the submission of proposals or recommendations to Congress; provisions imposing disclosure or reporting requirements; conditions and qualifications on executive appointments; and legislative veto provisions."[135]

In a signing statement attached to P.L. 107–77, Department of Commerce, Justice, State, Judiciary, and Related Agencies Act, President

DOI: 10.1057/9781137539625.0005

Bush clearly endorsed the unitary executive theory: "I note that Section 612 of the bill sets forth certain requirements regarding the organization of the Department of Justice's efforts to combat terrorism. This provision raises separation of powers concerns by improperly and unnecessarily *impinging upon my authority as President to direct the actions of the Executive Branch and its employees.* I therefore will construe the provision to avoid constitutional difficulties and preserve the separation of powers required by the Constitution."[136]

In a signing statement attached to the Enhanced Border Security and Visa Entry Reform Act of 2002, Bush again asserted executive autonomy, and rejected legislative mandates for coordination or consultation from Congress. He stated that such provisions would be treated as advisory only:

> Several actions of the Act raise constitutional concerns. Sections 2(6), 201 (c), and 202 (a) (3) purport to require the President to act through a specified assistant to the President in coordination or consultation with specified officers of the United States, agencies, or congressional committees. *The President's constitutional authority to supervise the unitary executive branch and take care that the laws be faithfully executed cannot be made by law subject to requirements to exercise those constitutional authorities through a particular member of the President's staff or in coordination or consultation with specified officers or elements of the Government.* Accordingly, the executive branch shall treat the purported requirements as precatory.[137]

In a signing statement attached to the Military Construction Appropriation Act of 2002, Bush asserted his constitutional authority to use emergency power:

> The U.S. Supreme Court has stated that the President's authority to classify and control access to information bearing on national security flows from the Constitution and does not depend upon a legislative grant of authority. Although the notice can be provided to Congress in most situations as a matter of comity, situations arise, especially in wartime, in which the President must act promptly under his constitutional grants of executive power and authority as Commander in Chief while protecting sensitive national security information. The executive branch shall construe these sections in a manner consistent with the President's constitutional authority.[138]

Bush's use of signing statements diverged from the historical precedent in the nature and sheer number of provisions challenged or objected to.[139] The key qualitative difference was President Bush's use of the signing statement to "emphatically endorse the unitariness of the executive branch."[140] He took very clear steps to assert sole presidential authority over the executive branch and the administration of policy initiatives, in particular, to assert his constitutional authority to prosecute the War on Terror.

The following signing statements further evidence Bush's logic regarding his constitutional authority to prosecute the war on terror and his support for the unitary executive theory. In a statement attached to the Homeland Security Act, Bush stated,

> The executive branch shall construe and carry out these provisions, as well as other provisions of the Act, including those in title II of the Act, in a manner consistent with the President's constitutional and statutory authorities to control access to and protect classified information, intelligence sources and methods, sensitive law enforcement information, and information the disclosure of which could otherwise harm the foreign relations or national security of the United States.[141]

In a signing statement attached to the Intelligence Reform and Terrorism Prevention Act of 2004, Bush objected to provisions requiring the executive branch to consult Congressional committees prior to executing the provision:

> Many provisions of the Act deal with the conduct of United States intelligence activities and the defense of the Nation, which are two of the most important functions of the Presidency. The executive branch shall construe the Act, including amendments made by the Act, in a manner consistent with the constitutional authority of the President to conduct the Nation's foreign relations, as Commander in Chief of the Armed Forces, and to supervise the unitary executive branch, which encompasses the authority to conduct intelligence operations.[142]

As suggested earlier, foreign affairs and points of executive emergency power are two of the primary areas in which President Bush has repeatedly raised constitutional objections and or challenges. For example, Bush remarked on provisions of the Syria accountability and Lebanese Sovereignty Restoration Act of 2003 that required the imposition of sanctions against Syria absent a presidential determination and certification that Syria had met certain conditions or that a determination of national security concerns justified a waiver of sanctions. The president declared,

> A law cannot burden or infringe the President's exercise of a core constitutional power by attaching conditions precedent to the use of that power. The executive branch shall construe and implement in a manner consistent with the President's constitutional authority to conduct the Nation's foreign affairs as the Commander in Chief, in particular with respect to the conduct of

foreign diplomats in the United States, the conduct of United States diplomats abroad, and the exportation of items and provisions of services necessary to the performance of official functions by United States government personnel abroad.[143]

Bush advocated the president's unilateral control over powers under Article II of the Constitution, in which he declared, "a law cannot burden or infringe upon the President's exercise of a core constitutional power." This constitutional power includes executive emergency power. Further, Bush advocated unilateral control over the execution of combating the emergency. He stated, "the executive branch shall construe and implement in a manner consistent with the President's constitutional authority to conduct the Nation's foreign affairs as the Commander in Chief."[144]

These signing statements imply that President Bush advocated both the Unitary Executive Theory and an interpretation of emergency power that suggests that a president may take any necessary actions to combat and dispel the crisis. Apparently, the president endorsed a theory of emergency power that suggests his powers during crisis were strong, swift, aggressive, and necessary when dealing with the crisis. Furthermore, the president seemed to suggest he was not bound solely by the Constitution, but was instead emboldened to protect, defend, and use all the power granted in the Constitution to deal with the crisis.

Discussion

Indubitably, the attacks of September 11, 2001, were an unprecedented emergency, and as such, President Bush bore the responsibility to respond to the crisis. He was confronted with determining the scope and magnitude of his authority to combat the crisis. I suggest President Bush fashioned Hamilton's theory of emergency power and Lincoln's necessity theory of executive power in time of crisis—making a new theory, a theory of an imperial presidency during time of crisis.

I think the most surprising conclusion about President Bush's actions is that they were limited. Bush didn't suspend habeas corpus, or shut down the Post Office (like Abraham Lincoln did), and he did not move the military without Congressional consent. President G. W. Bush did do extraordinary things; yet, he could have been even more brash. Bush's theory of executive emergency power, however, as John Yoo argued, based on Hamilton's theory, is overly stated, exaggerated, and at times

DOI: 10.1057/9781137539625.0005

simply misleading. Moreover, most of the anger or disagreement with Bush's use of such power is overstated primarily because it had been a long time since a president had used emergency powers. Would the same critics of President Bush's use of emergency power, who declared Bush was an "American Monarch," have made the same insinuation about Abraham Lincoln during the Civil War?[145]

Contemporary Americans are so far removed from the observation of emergency power, that they forget the potency and vigor of emergency power. The question remains, however; did President Bush have legal justification to use emergency power? A reassessment of the OLC's advice to the president will answer this question. According to the OLC, the lawyers concluded that President Bush had authority to act and repel the crisis based on an interpretation of Hamilton's writings. The OLC suggested that executive emergency powers are un-enumerated, derived from an interpretation of clauses within Article II of the Constitution.

The evidence suggests that Bush's interpretation of emergency power favored a strong, decisive executive, responsible for preserving the nation, and doing whatever was necessary to combat any threat posed toward the nation. Lead Attorney John Yoo constructed his entire hyper-unitary executive approach on Hamilton's Federalist writings. Is this theory congruent with Hamilton's argument for executive emergency power as being implicit within Article II of the Constitution? From the analysis conducted in this paper, I think one can assert with little reservation that John Yoo exaggerated Hamilton's theory and mischaracterized Hamilton's words to construct a hyper-unitary executive on steroids.

In Federalist No. 70, Hamilton argued for swift, energetic, and singular responses to crisis. He asserted that an executive must have the power to repel insurrection and invasions. Hamilton further suggested that an executive may have to act with "secrecy" and with "appropriate dispatch" to deal with the "insurrection."[146] With regard to responsiveness to the crisis, Bush advocated Hamilton's arguments in Federalist No. 70. Bush acted swiftly; the invasion of Afghanistan took place on September 23, 2001, just 12 days after the attacks. Bush authorized "secretive" investigations into potential terrorist activity both at home and abroad through the use of the Patriot Act and the detainment of enemy combatants at Guantanamo Bay. Both actions took effect by October 26, 2001, just 45 days after the September 11, 2001, attacks.

However, as evidenced through the analysis of the Federalist documents presented in this chapter, Hamilton never suggested that a

DOI: 10.1057/9781137539625.0005

president may act in discordance with the Congress and never advocated presidential authority to necessarily make war, or further still, to not seek consultation or oversight from Congress while he was using executive emergency power. Yoo often misconstrued Hamilton's argument to form this hyper-unitary approach, whereby the executive could violate the separation of powers doctrine. This hyper-unitary approach began during the Reagan years, only to be exploited, embellished, and intensified during the Bush years. Vice President Cheney and Secretary of Defense Rumsfeld were very strong advocates of a unitary executive, as many speeches and emails revealed after their times in office. Further, the OLC did not provide prudent legal reasoning to the President; rather they constructed a new theory of executive power that was hyper-unitary, cavalier, and unfettered.

The OLC argued that the attacks of September 11, 2001, constituted an invasion, hence warranting an executive response to the attack. The OLC argument further promoted that an executive may do whatever is necessary to deal with the crisis; implicitly, the executive may act without receiving Congressional approval.[147] The OLC further argued that the executive may act without seeking any Congressional consultation, or oversight in responding to the crisis.[148] This level of prerogative was not congruent with Hamilton's ideas. Hamilton was consistent in his argument that, even though an executive may have "broadened" power and responsibility during a crisis, the executive was not above any "magistrate" within the shared system of powers that is the federal government.[149]

Analysis of President Bush's signing statements produces a clear picture of his theory of emergency power that asserted presidential dominance over dealing with the crisis. Furthermore, Bush objected to any Congressional restraint or requirements placed on his actions, prior to his acting. Bush's assertion to act singularly was consistent with Hamilton's, but as evidenced in the signing statements Bush exceeded Hamilton's argument to suggest a complete disregard for Congressional consultation or oversight. Bush apparently believed he was "above magistrates" during a time of crisis, and was thus not consistent with Hamilton's argument.

How did Bush's lawyers' theory of executive emergency powers align with that of political philosophers? In light of the OLC opinions it would appear that Bush supported Locke's prerogative, cloaked in the implicit power argument of Hamilton. This is similar to Lincoln's interpretation

DOI: 10.1057/9781137539625.0005

of emergency power. Bush supported the idea that the president, while acting as commander-in-chief, must protect, defend, and preserve the Constitution, or what Bush called the "homeland." This logic recalls Locke's argument that emergency power, or prerogative, must be aimed at preserving the public good.

Bush strayed from the intellectual history of executive emergency power, and I think strayed from Lincoln, on the matter of separation of powers. According to the OLC opinions, the Bush administration advocated a Unitary Executive argument, that is, that the executive has unilateral control over the executive branch. This means the other branches have no oversight over the executive's prerogatives, and so support for a unitary executive makes the executive, in times of emergency, nothing less of an imperial president.

The OLC opinion argued for an interpretation of emergency power that supported a strong president in times of emergency. The power of commander-in-chief is the most critical. Accordingly, the OLC argued that in time of emergency, the president may respond to the crisis with whatever strength necessary because he has the power to command the army.[150] The president may conduct his actions without consultation or oversight from the Congress because he is solely responsible for protecting, preserving, and defending the Union. This logic is congruent with modern interpretation of the Unitary Executive Theory that suggests that presidents are inherently powerful, especially in times of emergency, and are not subject to other branches of the government's constraints or limitations on presidential prerogative. This advice supports a theory of executive emergency power favoring a centralization of power during a crisis—an imperial presidency based on the Hamiltonian American model. Therefore, Bush appears to have adopted an interpretation of executive emergency power very close to Lincoln's interpretation—of course outlined in Yoo's OLC argument, suggesting a president is imperialistic during a crisis. Further, the president is unfettered in determining what actions constitute emergency power. Luckily the events of September 11, 2001, did not evolve into a broader insurrection, because undoubtedly I think we may assert that the Bush presidency would have furthered actions inside the United States that would have shocked the conscience of the nation.

The Bush presidency interpretations' of emergency power conflict with Montesquieu's theory of separation of powers, even during an emergency. Montesquieu suggested that an executive may have to use

DOI: 10.1057/9781137539625.0005

emergency power, but still must respect the boundaries of separated powers.[151] Even in times of emergency the executive should respect the other branches of government.

Was the "war on terror" as much of a crisis as the Civil War? Obviously not; yet the way that the Bush presidency proffered their power and right to act during the crisis, one might think the nation was on the brink of a larger catastrophe. In terms of magnitude, the answer is obviously no. However, the OLC suggested that the potential "insurrection" of enemy combatants was unquantifiable, and, therefore, led the OLC to conclude that Bush's power was similar to Lincoln's necessary actions of emergency power during the Civil War.[152] But was the landscape similar enough to the Civil War circumstances to warrant broad authority, at least philosophically, after the attacks of September 11, 2001?

Unlike the early days of the Civil War, Congress was in session during the attacks. Bush initially sought Congressional authority for his actions, unlike Lincoln,[153] and received Congressional approval for his actions. The Military Authorization Act was passed in late September 2001, along with the Patriot Act. Did Bush use any power comparable to Lincoln's? The extraordinary renditions, and the detainment of enemy combatants at Guantanamo Bay may constitute a kind of habeas corpus suspension; the detainees are enemies of the state, however. The more important point to consider is that the OLC advised the president that he had broad authority if an "insurrection" actually occurred or intensified.[154]

However, the insurrection did not happen that prevented broader use of power during the Bush presidency. If a greater insurrection had occurred, then I do think President Bush would have embarked on a broader use of power that probably would have appeared similar to Lincoln's actions during the Civil War. Luckily that is not the case, though the unlucky ones are the enemy combatants. Bush clearly adopted and enacted a hyper-unitary approach, during a crisis, and executed power in a reckless, cavalier manner. Though, one might commend the administration for seeking Congressional approval for their actions, but recall, the information that the Congress had to make a decision was entirely owned and offered from the Administration. Presidents who are not bound by the rule of law, are not justifiable constitutional republican leaders. The president of the United States is never above the law, not even during an emergency. The President of the United States of America is not a law-maker rather he is to enforce the law, period. In time of crisis the President must seek legal permission to act, from

DOI: 10.1057/9781137539625.0005

the Congress, not from his Office of Legal Counsel. Determining who is an enemy combatant, determining rendition, determining interrogation, determining foreign espionage, and surveillance, are all functions of the legislative and executive prudence.

Cleary the Bush Administration favored the Hamiltonian approach to emergency power, whereby executive prerogative determined what and how to use emergency powers. The Bush prosecution of the war exemplified how powerful an executive might become during crisis as the Bush team expanded the meaning of laws, such as the Patriot Act, to enable broader interrogations and detentions of enemy combatants. In the end, the Bush presidency created presidential powers and executed such powers without Congressional input, and acted in ways unsupported by the Constitution. The evidence in this chapter draws the conclusion that the Constitution was not very important during the President's prosecution of the War on Terror.

Notes

1 Steven G. Calabresi and Christopher S. Yoo, *The Unitary Executive: Presidential Power from Washington to Bush* (New Haven, CT: Yale University Press, 2008). By reviewing the history of the republic and its corresponding theory, we find that modern interpretations have become more "extreme"; hence, previous presidents adopted a more nuanced interpretation.

2 Calabresi and Yoo, *The Unitary Executive*, 3–7.

3 Alexander Hamilton, Federalist No. 70, in Alexander Hamilton, James Madison, and John Jay, *The Federalist Papers*, 354–62 (New York: Bantam Press, 1982).

4 See especially John C. Yoo, *Memorandum Re: Authority for Use of Military Force to Combat Terrorist Activities Within the United States*, October 23, 2001, U.S. Department of Justice, Office of Legal Counsel.

5 Hamilton, Federalist No. 70.

6 Ibid.

7 Max Farrand, ed. *The Records of the Federal Convention of 1787* (New Haven, CT: Yale University Press, 1911), vol. 2, 537.

8 Ibid.

9 Hamilton, Federalist No. 70.

10 All of Hamilton's claims are drawn from Federalist No. 70. For an Anti-Federalist response, see George Clinton, Anti-Federalist No. 69, in Herbert J. Storing, and Murray Dry, *The Complete Anti-Federalist*, 115–17 (Chicago: University of Chicago Press, 1981).

DOI: 10.1057/9781137539625.0005

11 Hamilton, Federalist No. 70.

12 Edwin Meese, *With Reagan: The Inside Story* (Washington, DC: Regnery Gateway, 1992); and J. Yoo, *Memorandum Re: Authority for Use of Military Force to Combat Terrorist Activities Within the United States*, October 23, 2001.

13 Calabresi and Yoo, *The Unitary Executive*, 3–5.

14 I will explore constitutional objections to laws when I review presidential signing statements.

15 Calabresi and Yoo, *The Unitary Executive*, 3–5.

16 Ibid.

17 *Myers v. United States* (272 U.S. 52, 1926).

18 Calabresi and Yoo, *The Unitary Executive*, 3–5.

19 Michael Herz, "Imposing Unified Executive Branch Statutory Interpretation," *Cardozo Law Review* vol. 15, no. 1–2 (October 1993): 219–72, 252–53.

20 Elena Kagan, "Presidential Administration," *Harvard Law Review* vol. 114, no. 8 (June 2001): 2245–385, 2327.

21 Calabresi and Yoo, *The Unitary Executive*, 4–6.

22 Ibid., 5–8.

23 War Powers Resolution of 1973 (50 U.S.C. 1541–48).

24 Ibid.

25 Thomas Cronin, "An Imperiled Presidency," in *The Post-Imperial Presidency*, edited by Vincent Davis (New Brunswick, NJ: Transaction Books: 1980), 137–39.

26 Christopher Kelley, *Executing the Constitution: Putting the President Back into the Constitution* (Albany: State University of New York Press, 2006), 45–46.

27 Meese, *With Reagan*, 77.

28 Kelley, *Executing the Constitution*, 45–46.

29 Executive Order, signed March 13, 1937, 2 FR 619, March 16, 1937, revoked by Public Land Order 5887, May 18, 1981 (46 FR 28414), 46 Federal Register 131937, February 1981.

30 John Gattuso, *Washington D.C.: Know the City Like a Native* (Singapore: APA Publications, 2008).

31 Ibid.

32 Executive Order, signed March 13, 1937.

33 Joseph Cooper and William F. West, "Presidential Power and Republican Government: The Theory and Practice of OMB Review of Agency Rules," *The Journal of Politics* vol. 50, no. 4 (November 1988): 864–95, 873–75.

34 John Dean, "George W. Bush as the New Richard Nixon: Both Wiretapped Illegally, and Impeachably; Both Claimed That a President May Violate Congress' Laws to Protect National Security," FindLaw, December 30, 2005, http://writ.lp.findlaw.com/dean/20051230.html.

35 Meese, *With Reagan*; Calabresi and Yoo, *The Unitary Executive*; and J. Yoo, *Memorandum Re: Authority for Use of Military Force to Combat Terrorist Activities Within the United States*, October 23, 2001.

36 Hamilton, Federalist No. 70.

37 Ibid.

38 Alexander Hamilton, Federalist No. 77, in Hamilton, Madison, and Jay, *The Federalist Papers*, 388–92.

39 George W. Bush Interview, *60 Minutes*, CBS, November 17, 2010.

40 Nancy V. Baker, "The Attorney General as a Legal Policy Maker: Conflicting Loyalties," in *Government Lawyers: The Federal Legal Bureaucracy and Presidential Politics*, edited by Cornell W. Clayton (Lawrence: University of Kansas Press, 1995), 31–59.

41 Obtained from the U.S.DOJ OLC index.

42 Nelson Lund, "Guardians of the Presidency: The Office of the Counsel to the President and the Office of Legal Counsel," in Clayton, *Government Lawyers*, 209–57.

43 This is in addition to the Court overturning, in short, some of the OLC opinions regarding the removal and detainment of enemy combatants. See *Hamdi v. Rumsfeld* (542 U.S. 507 2004), and *Hamdan v. Rumsfeld 2006* (548 U.S. 557, 2006), (542 U.S. 507, 2004).

44 William. P. Barr, Testimony of William Barr, Hearing of the Commission on the Roles and Capabilities of the United States Intelligence Community, Room SD-106, Dirksen Senate Office Building, Washington, DC, Friday, January 19, 1996, transcript, 38.

45 Those bills that the administration advances are circulated to all interested agencies for comment. The OLC will get a bill only if the Office of Legislative Affairs seeks a legal review. Statement of Robert B. Shanks, Deputy Assistant Attorney General, Office of Legal Counsel, Before the Committee on Energy and Natural Resources, Subcommittee on Energy Conservation and Supply, U.S. Senate, Concerning Revised Constitution of American Samoa on May 8, 1984, 1–43.

46 Department of Justice, Office of Legal Counsel, http://www.justice.gov/olc/index.html.

47 Ibid.

48 J. Yoo, *Memorandum Re: Authority for Use of Military Force to Combat Terrorist Activities Within the United States*, October 23, 2001.

49 Ibid., 2.

50 Ibid.

51 J. Yoo, *Memorandum Re: Authority for Use of Military Force to Combat Terrorist Activities Within the United States*, October 23, 2001.

52 Ibid., 3.

53 Ibid., 2.

DOI: 10.1057/9781137539625.0005

54   Ibid., 3.

55   Ibid.

56   Ibid., 4.

57   Ibid.

58   Ibid., 3.

59   Alexander Hamilton, Federalist No. 23, in Hamilton, Madison, and Jay, *The Federalist Papers*, 111–15.

60   J. Yoo, *Memorandum Re: Authority for Use of Military Force to Combat Terrorist Activities Within the United States*, October 23, 2001, 5.

61   Ibid.

62   Ibid., 6.

63   Ibid.

64   John Yoo, *Crisis and Command: The History of Executive Power from George Washington to George W. Bush* (New York: Kaplan, 2009), ch. 1.

65   J. Yoo, *Memorandum Re: Authority for Use of Military Force to Combat Terrorist Activities Within the United States*, October 23, 2001, 6.

66   Ibid., 5.

67   Pacificus, "No. 1," in Herbert J. Storing, and Murray Dry (eds), *The Complete Anti-Federalist* (Chicago: University of Chicago Press, 1981), 23–27.

68   J. Yoo, *Memorandum Re: Authority for Use of Military Force to Combat Terrorist Activities Within the United States*, October 23, 2001, 7.

69   Alexander Hamilton, Federalist Paper No. 74, in Hamilton, Madison, and Jay, *The Federalist Papers*, 374–76.

70   J. Yoo, *Memorandum Re: Authority for Use of Military Force to Combat Terrorist Activities Within the United States*, October 23, 2001, 9.

71   Ibid.

72   Ibid.

73   Hamilton, Federalist No. 23.

74   Ibid.

75   Ibid.

76   This is demonstrated most notably in Hamilton, Federalist No. 70.

77   Alexander Hamilton, Federalist No. 24, in Hamilton, Madison, and Jay, *The Federalist Papers*, 116–20.

78   Alexander Hamilton, Federalist No. 25, in Hamilton, Madison, and Jay, *The Federalist Papers*, 120–25.

79   J. Yoo, *Memorandum Re: Authority for Use of Military Force to Combat Terrorist Activities Within the United States*, October 23, 2001, 7.

80   Hamilton, Federalist No. 25.

81   Ibid.

82   Alexander Hamilton, Federalist No. 26, Hamilton, Madison, and Jay, *The Federalist Papers*, 125–30.

DOI: 10.1057/9781137539625.0005

83 Stephen G. Bradbury, Memorandum for the Files Re: October 23, 2001 OLC Opinion Addressing the Domestic Use of Military Force to Combat Terrorist Activities, October 6, 2008, U.S. Department of Justice, 1–2.

84 Ibid., 2.

85 Patrick F. Philbin, Legality of the Use of Military Commissions to Try Terrorists, November 6, 2001, U.S. Department of Justice.

86 Ibid., 7.

87 Jay S. Bybee, Memorandum Re: the President's Power as Commander in Chief to Transfer Captured Terrorists to the Control and Custody of Foreign Nations, March 13, 2002, U.S. Department of Justice.

88 Jay S. Bybee, Memorandum for John Rizzo, Acting General Counsel of the Central Intelligence Agency, Interrogation of al Qaeda Operative, August 1, 2002, U.S. Department of Justice, 2–3.

89 Ibid., 2–4.

90 Ibid., 2–3.

91 John Yoo, *Memorandum Re; Constitutionality of Amending Foreign Intelligence Surveillance Act to Change the "Purpose" Standard for Searches*, September 25, 2001.2–4.

92 NBC/Washington Post Poll, *Wall Street Journal*, September 17, 2001.

93 J. Yoo, *Memorandum Re: Authority for Use of Military Force to Combat Terrorist Activities Within the United States*, October 23, 2001.

94 Authorization for Use of Military Force, September 18, 2001, Public Law 107–40 (S. J. RES. 23) 107th Congress.

95 See Louis Fisher, *Presidential War Power*, 2nd ed. (Lawrence: University Press of Kansas, 1995); Garry Wills, *Bomb Power: The Modern Presidency and the National Security State* (New York: Penguin Press, 2010).

96 Authorization for Use of Military Force, September 18, 2001.

97 J. Yoo, *Memorandum Re: Authority for Use of Military Force to Combat Terrorist Activities Within the United States*, October 23, 2001.

98 Authorization for Use of Military Force, September 18, 2001, 5.

99 Ibid.

100 George W. Bush, Remarks on Arrival at the White House and an Exchange with Reporters, September 16, 2001, http://www.presidency.ucsb.edu/mediaplay.php?id=63346&admin=43.

101 Ibid.

102 Some also suggest that this can possibly be attributed to the continuation of Congress's willingness to allow the president to "make war." See Fisher, *Presidential War Power* and Wills, *Bomb Power*.

103 George W. Bush, Address before a Joint Session of the Congress on the United States Response to the Terrorist Attacks of September 11, September 20, 2001, http://www.presidency.ucsb.edu/mediaplay.php?id=64731&admin=43.

DOI: 10.1057/9781137539625.0005

104 Authorization for Use of Military Force, September 18, 2001.

105 Ibid.

106 See Fisher, *Presidential War Power* and Wills, *Bomb Power*.

107 David Currie, "Rumors of War: Presidential and Congressional War Powers," *University of Chicago Law Review* vol. 67, no. 1 (2000): 1–40.

108 Bob Woodward, *Bush at War* (New York Simon and Shuster, 2002), 15–30.

109 Ibid., 23–35.

110 Ibid., 15–30.

111 Howard Ball, *The U.S.A Patriot Act of 2001: Balancing Civil Liberties and National Security: A Reference Handbook* (Santa Barbara, CA: ABC-CLIO, 2004).

112 Fred Barbash, "Justices Reject Appeal Over the Secret 9–11 Detainees," *Washington Post*, January 12, 2004.

113 Timothy Lynch, *Breaking the Vicious Cycle: Preserving Our Liberties while Fighting Terrorism* (Washington, DC: CATO Institute, June 26, 2002), Policy Analysis 443.

114 James Risen, *State of War: The Secret History of the CIA and the Bush Administration* (New York: Free Press, 2006), 42–44.

115 Ibid., 37, 43. See Patriot Act, Title II, Section 215, under "sneak and peek" and "roving wiretaps" provisions, both of which allow federal agents to secure the gathering of terrorist information without first requesting a specified warrant.

116 J. Yoo, *Memorandum Re: Authority for Use of Military Force to Combat Terrorist Activities Within the United States*, October 23, 2001, 6.

117 Kate Martin, "Legal Detainment?," Center for National Security Studies, 2004, in *SAIS Review* vol. 29, no. 1 (Winter–Spring 2004), 6–7.

118 J. Yoo, *Memorandum Re: Authority for Use of Military Force to Combat Terrorist Activities Within the United States*, October 23, 2001, 6.

119 U.S. Department of Justice, Department of Justice Inspector General Issues Report on Treatment of Aliens Held on Immigration Charges in Connection with the Investigation of the September 11 Terrorist Attacks, June 2, 2003, http://www.justice.gov/oig/special/0306/press.pdf.

120 Ibid.

121 John Mayer, "Outsourcing Torture: The Secret History of America's Extraordinary Rendition Program," *New Yorker*, February 14, 2005.

122 *Amnesty International.* "USA: Below the Radar: Secret Flights to Torture: and 'Disappearance.'" April 2006. http://www.amnesty.org/en/library/info/AMR51/051/2006.

123 Mayer, "Outsourcing Torture."

124 Risen, *State of War*, 28.

125 Phillip J. Cooper, "George W. Bush, Edgar Allen Poe, and the Use and Abuse of Presidential Signing Statements," *Presidential Studies Quarterly* vol. 35, no. 3 (September 2005): 515–32, 517.

DOI: 10.1057/9781137539625.0005

126 Christopher May, "Presidential Defiance of Unconstitutional Laws: Reviving the Royal Prerogative," *Hastings Constitutional Legislative Quarterly* vol. 21 (1994): 932. President Jackson was the first to issue a signing statement, and John Tyler was first to use the statement to question the constitutionality of the statute submitted to him. Letter from John Tyler to the House of Representatives, June 25, 1842, in James D. Richardon (ed.), *A Compilation of the Messages and Papers of the Presidents, 1842* (Washington, DC: Government Printing Office, 1897).

127 T. J. Halstead, Congressional Research Service, "Presidential Signing Statements: Constitutional and Institutional Implications" (Washington, DC: Congressional Research Service, Library of Congress, 2007).

128 Neil Kinkopf, "Index of Presidential Signing Statements, 2001–2007," *American Constitution Society of Law and Policy*, August 2007.

129 Wills, *Bomb Power*, 219; Charlie Savage. *Takeover: The Return of the Imperial Presidency and the Subversion of American Democracy* (New York: Little, Brown, 2007), 35; and Halstead, Congressional Research Service, "Presidential Signing Statements."

130 U.S.A Patriot Improvement and Reauthorization Act of 2005, P/L 109–177; George W. Bush, Statement upon Signing H.R. 3199, March 9, 2006.

131 George W. Bush, Address to the Nation, September 21, 2001, President Bush's Library Archives, Arlington Texas.

132 J. Yoo, *Memorandum Re: Authority for Use of Military Force to Combat Terrorist Activities Within the United States*, October 23, 2001, 6.

133 Cooper, "George W. Bush, Edgar Allen Poe, and the Use and Abuse of Presidential Signing Statements," 517.

134 Curtis A. Bradley, Eric A. Posner, "Presidential Signing Statements and Executive Power," *Constitutional Commentary* 23 (2006), 307, 323.

135 Cooper, "George W. Bush, Edgar Allen Poe, and the Use and Abuse of Presidential Signing Statements," 522.

136 Presidential Signing Statement, P.L. 107–77, *Weekly Compilation of Presidential Documents* 37 (2001), 1724.

137 Enhanced Border Security and Visa Entry Form Act of 2002, P.L. 107–173, signed June 2002, *Weekly Compilation of Presidential Documents* 38 (2002), 822.

138 Military Construction Appropriation Act of 2002, P.L. 106–52, *Weekly Compilation of Presidential Documents* 38 (2002), 1836.

139 Cooper, "George W. Bush, Edgar Allen Poe and the Use and Abuse of Presidential Signing Statements"; Christopher Yoo, Steven G. Calabresi, and Anthony J. Colangelo, "The Unitary Executive in the Modern Era, 1945–2004," *Iowa Law Review* vol. 90, no. 2 (2005): 601, 722.

140 Yoo, Calabresi, and Colangelo, "The Unitary Executive in the Modern Era," 722.

DOI: 10.1057/9781137539625.0005

141 Homeland Security Act, P.L. 107–296, *Weekly Compilation of Presidential Documents* (2002), 2093.

142 Intelligence Reform and Terrorism Prevention Act of 2004, P.L. 108–458, *Weekly Compilation of Presidential Documents* (2004), 2993.

143 George W. Bush, Statement upon Signing the Syria Accountability and Lebanese Sovereignty Restoration Act of 2003, December 12, 2003.

144 George W. Bush, Statement upon Signing U.S.A Patriot Improvement and Reauthorization Act of 2005, P/L. 109–177, H.R. 3199, March 9, 2006.

145 Wills, *Bomb Power*, 145–63.

146 Hamilton, Federalist No. 70.

147 J. Yoo, *Memorandum Re: Authority for Use of Military Force to Combat Terrorist Activities Within the United States*, October 23, 2001, 4–7.

148 Ibid., 6.

149 Alexander Hamilton, Federalist No. 76, in Hamilton, Madison, and Jay, *The Federalist Papers*.

150 J. Yoo, *Memorandum Re: Authority for Use of Military Force to Combat Terrorist Activities Within the United States*, October 23, 2001.

151 Montesquieu, Spirit of the Laws, in Michael Morgan, ed., *Classics of Moral and Political Theory* (Indianapolis, IN: Hackett Publishing Co., 1992), 431–40.

152 J. Yoo, *Memorandum Re: Authority for Use of Military Force to Combat Terrorist Activities Within the United States*, October 23, 2001, 13.

153 Initially Lincoln could not seek congressional authority because Congress was out of session. However, in his message to Congress on July 4, 1861, he made clear that he felt that Congress would support all his actions, which they did.

154 J. Yoo, *Memorandum Re: Authority for Use of Military Force to Combat Terrorist Activities Within the United States*, October 23, 2001.

DOI: 10.1057/9781137539625.0005

3

President Obama, the Nobel Peace Prize Winner and the War on Terror

Abstract: *President Obama had vowed, as a candidate for the US presidency, not to push America into any new wars. Likewise, he vowed to make peace with the Arab-Islamic world and to end the War on Terror. In this chapter I examine the President's use of executive emergency power and make a startling discovery that the Nobel Peace Prize winning President Obama is actually just a ruthless, if not more, than the cowboy President G. W. Bush.*

DePlato, Justin. *American Presidential Power and the War on Terror: Does the Constitution Matter?* New York: Palgrave Macmillan, 2015. DOI: 10.1057/9781137539625.0006.

The War on Terror has raged on since September 11, 2001. In 2008, President Obama was elected with a rather large mandate, of which, the electorate wanted him to end the wars in Afghanistan and Iraq. Obama, obliged, and actively campaigned for ending the wars while chastising his predecessor President G. W. Bush for starting wars of choice. In fact, Senator Obama and Senator Biden overtly chastised the Bush presidency repeatedly for over-extending their powers during the War on Terror and even suggested in Senate floor speeches that if the PRISM program existed, such an occurrence of presidential prerogative power would be an impeachable offense. Of course, history will turn out to show us that President Obama is nothing like the Senator Obama, and the world will see the PRISM program during his time in Office; Obama will advocate for the PRISM program rather than impeach the President.

In this chapter, I examine and highlight President Obama's justification and the use of emergency power over the first six years of his presidency. Remarkably, the President's use of power appears very similar to his predecessor. President Obama will orchestrate the assassination of over 2,000 enemy combatants, will maintain Guantanamo Bay prison, will orchestrate several "new" campaigns in Iraq, will continue to use whatever means he deems necessary to define and interrogate enemy combatants, will unilaterally rewrite and limitedly enforce the Affordable Care Act of 2011, and most shockingly, will engage the United States in a new war front, namely on the War on Terror, in Syria, taking on the new formed army of ISIS (ISIL).

Prior to Barack Obama's election to Office he consistently chastised President G. W. Bush. In particular, President Obama's complaints were that President G. W. Bush overused his prerogative powers to determine what and how to use power to combat the War on Terror. In January 2009, shortly after taking Office (that same month), President Obama's Office of Legal Counsel issued a scathing memo calling for an immediate "halt" and "repudiation" of all former presidential legal opinions regarding presidential power authored during the Bush presidency.[1] Further, the Obama campaign stressed a need to stop doing what G. W. Bush was going to prosecute the War on Terror. This call to stop action was rooted in repudiating Bush's decisions to detain enemy combatants at Guantanamo Bay, stop the enhanced interrogation methods—especially waterboarding—to reconsider the surveillance program, and to limit the use of drones to assassinate enemy combatants.

In December 2009, President Obama was awarded the Nobel Peace Prize, and in his acceptance speech he continued to chastise world leaders who did not adhere to a strict rule of law when determining how to

DOI: 10.1057/9781137539625.0006

handle terrorism. He went on to support "just war" theories that maintained a "restrained" approach to combat and his speech reinforced the general precepts that war is at times necessary to protect the innocent but this does not include doing whatever is believed to be necessary to combat a crisis.[2] Further, President Obama gave an international address in Cairo, Egypt, in July 2009 in which he again pledged to the world that the United States was no longer pursuing its aggressive, hostile, and combative approach to handling terrorism; rather, America would pursue a legal, tempered approach.[3] I think many have forgotten that President Obama presented himself as the calm tempered leader and that President G. W. Bush was at times hasty and decided to use "boots on the ground" too quickly; rather, President Obama would deliberate more, build more consensus, and would inform the Arab Muslim world that America does not hate Islam. In so doing, the Obama strategy was to build a new bridge of appeasement with the hostile enemies in the hope that the enemy would stop their brutal attacks against America and the West.

The War on Terror has poised a surprising philosophical moment in American foreign policy and presidential power. In just 13 years, the United States electorate has elected one Republican and one Democrat president. The Republican, upon leaving Office, was looked at as a "cowboy," reckless in his pursuit of terror abroad. The Left argued that G. W. Bush was creating more enemies by starting wars in the Middle East, in particular, Iraq. Many thought the election of President Obama, who would be more tempered, deliberate, and would address the Arab Muslim world more respectfully, would foster a different outcome and would potentially end the War on Terror. Unfortunately for the Left, President Obama is no different than President G. W. Bush. In an earlier book I defined the rise of the modern presidency in light of the War on Terror as a new form of presidency, which I termed as the cavalier presidency. President Obama, just like President G. W. Bush, is as cavalier and as reckless in justifying, determining, and using his emergency power. Both Presidents, one a Republican and one a Democrat, have used an unfettered prerogative to determine what and how to use emergency presidential power. Contrary to President Obama's passivity and rhetoric, he is no exception. As the following facts demonstrate, President Obama has maintained and continues to support a total war on terror and tends to be a cavalier president rather than a restrained rule-abiding executive:

▸ In Executive Order 13618, President Obama declared that the US government may spy on American citizens through the

DOI: 10.1057/9781137539625.0006

National Security Agency PRISM program. This program collects metadata on all Americans, provided by warrant, from all major telecommunications and social media networks in the USA. Although the intent is not to violate the privacy of law-abiding citizens, it nonetheless sweeps data on all law-abiding citizens, essentially rendering all Americans as potential suspects in the War on Terror.

▸ The Obama administration continues to use drone strikes against enemy combatants of the state, and the executive branch is still the sole branch of government authorized to determine not only whether a foreigner or American citizen is an enemy combatant but also when, where, and how the US government attacks the enemy combatant, all with no Congressional oversight. Estimates indicate that during President Obama's time in Office he has ordered the execution, via drone strike, of over 2,000 people.

▸ The Obama administration's Department of Justice issued warrants to seize journalist records in an investigation pursuing a "mole" in the Associate Press. The warrant was unprecedented, sweeping a collection of all credentials and hard drives, with no notice. The President supported the action in the name of national security. As of date, the mole has not been found.

▸ President Obama has left Guantanamo Bay open and operating.

The President's signature legislative achievement was the Affordable Care Act of 2011. Under the Act, all Americans would be mandated to purchase health insurance or face a penalty for not doing so. The President sought to achieve universal health care for all Americans and the Left commended him for his actions. The Act, however, in its implementation was very messy. In the end, the President waived or delayed parts of the law over 10 times. In some cases, the mandate was eliminated altogether. The President's unilateral action to delay mandates or provisions of the law is highly unusual and, frankly, unconstitutional. The jury is still out on the future of the Act, but clearly some of the President's executive orders changing, delaying, or eliminating the mandates will be challenged in the court of law.

Finally, on September 10, 2014, President Obama addressed the nation and outlined his desire to attack ISIS (ISIL), an Islamic army, mostly Sunnis, who want to establish a new Islamic caliphate in the Middle East. The army had, prior to the address, seized large portions of Syria

DOI: 10.1057/9781137539625.0006

and Northern Iraq. In addition to their land conquest, the army had killed over 5,000 innocent soldiers or civilians and was embarking on a strategy of beheading western operatives, journalists, and aid workers as a way to deter western military intervention. President Obama declared a "total" war against them in which the United States would "denegade" and "destroy" ISIS wherever they exist. The speech reminded most of President G. W. Bush's early speeches against Al-Qaeda. President Obama made clear that no nation may harbor ISIS and that ISIS is not safe anywhere in the world. This statement clearly avers the Bush's Doctrine.

Americans must be scratching their heads over President Obama. The nation is going to embark on another Middle East war, and this time the leader is the Nobel Peace Prize winning Obama, not the cowboy Bush. I suppose we can assert that the War on Terror is not a function of partisanship or choice, rather, it is an endless war, where even the dove becomes a hawk. Our nation should be weary that in a short six years the War on Terror has enveloped a dovish democrat President into a new war front that may be bloodier and more endless than anything President G. W. Bush embarked upon. In summation, both President Obama and President Bush have adopted the implied the model of emergency powers, whereby executive prerogative determines what and how to use emergency power. In both instances, the Presidents are not acquiescing to Constitutional enumerations, rather they are ignoring the Constitution and establishing precedents that are not expressed in the Constitution. In essence, the Presidents are making the Constitution meaningless as the Government chooses their own forms of power, not bound or enumerated in the Constitution. The kings of America are alive and well in their pursuit of terrorists.

Notes

1   Office of Legal Counsel, "RE: Status of Certain OLC Opinion Issued in the Aftermath of the Terrorist Attacks of September 11, 2001," US Department of Justice, January 15, 2009.
2   Speech on September 10, 2014.
3   Ibid.

DOI: 10.1057/9781137539625.0006

Conclusion: The Republic Is in Danger

Abstract: *America's Republic is at war with an enigmatic enemy. The War on Terror is in its 14th year, with no end in sight. America has been under emergency laws since September 11, 2001 and the US President has ordered the assassination of more people, than at any time in American history. The USA might call itself a constitutional republic, yet, in time of war, and in this case a War on Terror, the US Republic behaves much more like an authoritative monarchy, whereby the executive decides which war to wage and how to wage it. This conclusion is startling, but consistent with broader liberal democratic theory. In war, the law is silent and this is true with the US Republic.*

DePlato, Justin. *American Presidential Power and the War on Terror: Does the Constitution Matter?* New York: Palgrave Macmillan, 2015. DOI: 10.1057/9781137539625.0007.

DOI: 10.1057/9781137539625.0007

In this book I examined the American presidential theory of emergency power in light of America's most complicated emergency, namely, their declared War on Terror. In so doing, I examined the Founders' and Framers' debates over the construction of Article II of the Constitution and the establishment of executive emergency power. First, I found that Presidents favor Hamilton's theory of executive energy and Locke's assertions of prerogative power and argue that the power is implicit in Article II of the Constitution. Thereby, this claim asserts that the Constitution does matter in times of crisis.

The Federalists claimed that Presidents do have the entitled right to command the army in times of crisis, which means they have the right to assert the means of war (i.e., interrogation). Further, they have the entitled right to "defend the Constitution" using the competent powers proscribed to them in the Constitution, of which military power is included. In addition, the Vesting Clause clearly establishes that there are implied powers in Article II of the Constitution, which is accomplished by not stating "powers herein reserved to the Executive," and in times of crisis, the actions taken against the Union are always criminal. Therefore, the Executive has the entitled right to "take care" that the laws are faithfully executed, which implies the use of means to pursue criminal activity.

While the Anti-Federalists argued fervently against the rise of a single president with competent powers, they lost the debate and in the end the American president, via the vesting clause, the Commander-in-Chief clause, the Oath Clause and the Take Care Clause, is empowered with extraordinary powers in times of crisis. Coupling all of these clauses together, Presidents G. W. Bush and Obama agree that they can do whatever is necessary to protect the USA because they are obligated to defend the Constitution (oath clause), they must faithfully execute the law (take care clause), they must command the army (commander-in-chief clause), and the vesting clause suggests that some powers are implied in Article II, of which emergency power is one of them.

What is most interesting about the debate over emergency power, at the founding of the nation, was the Anti-Federalist fervent concern that presidents, when using their competent powers, would easily appear and be confused with monarchs. The contemporary strife is riddled with executive over reach. My fellow scholar, Professor Tully, tells us that the President in 2014 is acting similar to that of a royal British Monarch. There is little to no doubt that the use of executive power and prerogative

DOI: 10.1057/9781137539625.0007

has changed the Executive Office from a servant of the people to the master of the law and the people.

The Anti-Federalists were very correct when they realized that executive power would only increase with time, especially in times of crisis. Both Presidents G. W. Bush and Obama have gone well beyond the scope of the written law. G. W. Bush redefined interrogation methods, detained rendition people at will, and ignored civil liberties if the nation was at risk. President Obama has killed thousands in the name of protecting the nation, denied due process to detained enemy combatants, and has rewritten the Affordable Care Act so many times that the law is a shell of its original form. The "royal brute" of England, as the Anti-Federalists coined King George during and after the revolution, would admire the proud executive prerogative of modern American presidents. Therefore, they argued for an expressed power, not an implied model of executive emergency power.

Does the president have such executive authority? This is a very good question and one that this book spent a lot of time answering. As stated, the Federalists through the pen of Hamilton and the lifting of Locke's "prerogative power" theory make the case that an Executive does have implied emergency powers. Therefore, if you agree with implied powers, then, sure, you can make the case that executive emergency powers exist. But this is fool's logic, simply because you are acknowledging that something implied exists. Clearly, the Constitution does not afford any person, be it the president, or a citizen of the USA to violate the law, period. In so doing, the president is acting above the law, which is a violation of the Supremacy clause of the Constitution. As Thomas Paine said so correctly in 1775, "In America the Law is King."

The Founders knew that emergencies need strong powerful responses and they correctly afford that power in the Constitution. Congress has the right to suspend habeas corpus in times of insurrection and emergency, not the executive. Congress always has the right to make laws; therefore, Congress can legislate the War on Terror, rather than executive fiat dictating military deployment and intrusions on civil liberties.

The two presidencies tasked with the complicated and delicate responsibility of defending Americans and fighting the War on Terror, Bush and Obama, have both adopted the implied model of executive emergency power. Both men have argued and used their prerogative to determine and use emergency power. Both presidencies have failed to consult the Constitutional enumerations to determine their power; rather they are

DOI: 10.1057/9781137539625.0007

using their own "king"-like prerogative. This evidence supports the argument that in the War on Terror, the Constitution is rather useless as a document used to determine the appropriate powers or scope of Executive or Federal Power.

How can any American citizen or scholar, who has read the Constitution and understands it, sit in the twenty-first century and agree with the executive fiats over the past 13 years. Our Constitution and our reverence for the law are looking like childish folly overseas. We are nothing if we are not reverent of the law. When you sit outside the great halls of justice and you teach your child about respecting the law, and he looks at you and says, "but daddy, sometimes the executive breaks the law, why is that ok"? And you simply say "because of the circumstances," then the rule of law is dead and our children will grow up in America where they will be accustomed to a king, rather than a Constitutional President of a Republic ruled by the law. Yes, some might argue the power is implied, yet thinking so is a very dangerous and undemocratic conclusion.

Therefore, I suggest an important solution to the implied theory paradigm of executive emergency powers. Simply make the power expressed. The US government should adopt an amendment to the Federal Constitution that enumerates executive emergency power. Insert recommendation here.

A major conclusion drawn from this research is not only that Presidents are breaking the law or violating the Constitution, but that the act to use and justify executive emergency power is not a function of party. President G. W. Bush, a republican, and President Obama, a democrat, prove that both parties are in agreement when it comes to doing whatever is necessary to save the Republic, even if that means endorsing the writing of laws such as the Patriot Act, ignoring the War Powers Act, using unmanned drones to assassinate people abroad, enhanced interrogations (violating international treaties), detaining combatants at will, extraordinary rendition, and spying on all Americans, along with seizing journalists' archives and data. To think, that we live in a country that prides itself on freedom, and that I just wrote a list of actions that violate freedom, the hypocrisy is incredulous. Yes, these Presidents might argue that their emergency powers are implied in Article II, but saying so does not make them real, or rather Constitutional. If the powers are easily understood as implied, then why not amend the Constitution to enumerate such powers? I think the solution to this problem is to amend the Constitution to enumerate the powers. Granting an executive such a

DOI: 10.1057/9781137539625.0007

power as emergency, in times of crisis, as implied is a dangerous concept, for obvious historical reasons.

There is no doubt that crisis management is hard and saving every American life is the paramount responsibility of the government, but they must do so legally, not at the expense of the Constitution and civil liberties.

A second conclusion drawn from this research is that public opinion, after the attacks of September 11, 2001, and since emergency powers were enacted, informs us that the American people are tolerating the trampling of the Constitution, and that most Americans agree that sacrificing some liberty for safety is necessary. According to a Gallup Poll, 2012, 75 percent of Americans agree that the president must do whatever is necessary to fight terrorism, even if it means breaking the laws. If only Benjamin Franklin was alive to give us his take on that poll, after all, he famously remarked, "if you are willing to exchange liberty for safety, then you never deserved liberty to begin with." Our nation is changing because our Presidents are too powerful, and what is most concerning is that the American people are not bothered by such developments. The people seem to think that the President has their best interest at heart, be it fighting terrorists, providing universal health care, or may be granting amnesty for all immigrants here illegally. Yet, our nation is not a monarchy; rather we are in a nation ruled by the law, not by men. However, the contemporary landscape makes the statement very clear that executive fiat is becoming the norm, crisis management the norm, and unbounded, unbridled executive power the norm, welcome not to a Constitutional Republic, but to a monarchy.

Americans must realize that they are safest not when government is drastically powerful and acting with no limitations, rather they are safest when government is constrained and the people are free to pursue legal ends without government intrusion. We can write laws to combat terrorism that do not violate our liberties, or make us appear contradictory in the eyes of the world. A great president, the one who will win this war, will be the one to restrain his power, and to make Congress write laws to protect and promote American reverence for the law. Our nation may continue to pursue this endless war on terror; in so doing, though we may realize we are not just destroying the enemy abroad, we may in fact start destroying ourselves from within. The Kings of America are alive and well in their pursuit of the terrorists.

DOI: 10.1057/9781137539625.0007

References

Adler, David Gray. "Presidential Power and Foreign Affairs in the Bush Administration: The Use and Abuse of Alexander Hamilton." *Presidential Studies Quarterly* 40, no. 3 (September 2010): 531–44.

Amnesty International. "USA: Below the Radar: Secret Flights to Torture: and 'Disappearance.'" April 2006. www.amnesty.org/en/library/info/AMR51/051/2006.

Aristotle. "Aristotle's Politics"', in *Classics of Moral and Political Theory,* edited by Morgan (Indianapolis, IN: Hackett, 2001).

Bailey, Jeremy. *Thomas Jefferson and Executive Power.* Cambridge, New York: Cambridge University Press, 2007.

Baker, Nancy V. "The Attorney General as a Legal Policy Maker: Conflicting Loyalties," in *Government Lawyers: The Federal Legal Bureaucracy and Presidential Politics,* edited by Cornell W. Clayton (Lawrence: University of Kansas Press, 1995), 31–59.

Baldwin, Leland D. *Whisky Rebels: The Story of Frontier Uprising.* Pittsburgh, PA: University of Pittsburgh Press, 1939.

Ball, Howard. *The USA Patriot Act of 2001: Balancing Civil Liberties and National Security: A Reference Handbook.* Santa Barbara, CA: ABC-CLIO, 2004.

Barbash, Fred. "Justices Reject Appeal over the Secret 9–11 Detainees." *Washington Post* January 12, 2004.

Boyd, Steven R. *The Whiskey Rebellion: Past and Present Perspectives.* Westport, CT: Greenwood Press, 1985.

Brackenridge, Henry M. *History of the Western Insurrection, 1794.* New York: Arno Press, 1969.

DOI: 10.1057/9781137539625.0008

Bradbury, Stephen G. Memorandum for the Files Re: October 23, 2001 OLC Opinion Addressing the Domestic Use of Military Force to Combat Terrorist Activities. October 6, 2008. U.S. Department of Justice.

Bradley, A. and Eric A. Posner. "Presidential Signing Statements and Executive Power." *Constitutional Commentary* 23 (2006): 307–64.

Brands, H. W. *Andrew Jackson: His Life and Times*. New York: Doubleday, 2005.

Bryant, Irving. "Madison Encouraged the War Movement," in *The Causes of the War of 1812: National Honor or National Interest?* edited by Bradford Perkins (New York: Holt, Rinehart and Winston, 1962), 104–107.

Bryce, James. *The American Commonwealth, vol. I, The National Government, the State Government*. Indianapolis, IN: Liberty Fund, 1995.

Bush, George W. Address before a Joint Session of the Congress on the United States Response to the Terrorist: Attacks of September 11. September 20, 2001. www.presidency.ucsb.edu/mediaplay.php?id=64731&admin=43.

_____ Interview, *60 Minutes*. CBS, November 17, 2010.

_____ Remarks on Arrival at the White House and an Exchange with Reporters. September 16, 2001. www.presidency.ucsb.edu/mediaplay.php?id=63346&admin=43.

Bybee, Jay S. Memorandum for John Rizzo, Acting General Counsel of the Central Intelligence Agency, Interrogation of al-Qaeda Operative. August 1, 2002. U.S. Department of Justice.

_____ Memorandum Re: The President's Power as Commander in Chief to Transfer Captured Terrorists to the Control and Custody of Foreign Nations. March 13, 2002. U.S. Department of Justice.

Calabresi, Steven. "Advice to the Next Conservative President of the United States." *Harvard Journal of Law and Public Policy* 24, pt. 2 (Spring 2001): 369–80.

Calabresi, Steven G. and Christopher S. Yoo. *The Unitary Executive: Presidential Power from Washington to Bush*. New Haven, CT: Yale University Press, 2008.

Carpenter, Allen Harmon. "Military Government of Southern Territory, 1861–1865." *Annual Report*. Washington, DC: Government Printing Office, 1900.

Clayton, Cornell W. (ed.) *Government Lawyers: The Federal Legal Bureaucracy and Presidential Politics*. Lawrence: University of Kansas Press, 1995.

DOI: 10.1057/9781137539625.0008

Cooper, Joseph, and William West. "Presidential Power and Republican Government: The Theory and Practice of OMB Review of Agency Rules." *The Journal of Politics* 50, no. 4 (November 1988): 864–95.

Cooper, Phillip J. "George W. Bush, Edgar Allen Poe, and the Use and Abuse of Presidential Signing Statements." *Presidential Studies Quarterly* 35, no. 3 (September 2005): 515–32.

Corwin, Edward. *The Office and Powers of the Presidency* (Oxford University Press, Oxford England, 1935)

Corwin, Edward Samuel, Randall Walton Bland, Theodore T. Hindson, and J. W. Peltason, *The President: Office and Powers, 1787–1984: History and Analysis of Practice and Opinion.* New York: New York University Press, 1984.

Cronin, Thomas. "An Imperiled Presidency," in *The Post-Imperial Presidency,* edited by Vincent Davis (New Brunswick, NJ: Transaction Books, 1980).

Cunningham, Noble E. *The Process of Government under Jefferson.* Princeton, NJ: Princeton University Press, 1978.

Currie, David "Rumors of War: Presidential and Congressional War Powers." *University of Chicago Law Review* 67, no. 1 (2000): 1–40.

Dean, John. "George W. Bush as the New Richard Nixon: Both Wiretapped Illegally, and Impeachably; Both Claimed That a President May Violate Congress' Laws to Protect National Security." Find Law. December 30, 2005. writ.lp.findlaw.com/dean/20051230.html.

Ehrenberg, Victor. *From Solon to Socrates: Greek History and Civilization During the 6th and 5th Centuries B.C.* London: Routledge, 1996.

Farrand, Max. (ed.) *The Records of the Federal Convention of 1787.* New Haven, CT: Yale University Press, 1911.

Fehrenbacher, Don Edward. *The Civil War: Rebellion to Reconstruction.* Princeton, NJ: Princeton University Press, 1950.

Fisher, Louis. *Presidential War Power,* 2nd ed. Lawrence: University Press of Kansas, 2004.

Fisher, S. G. "The Suspension of Habeas Corpus during the War of the Rebellion." *Political Science Quarterly* 3, no. 3 (1888): 454–88.

Fitzpatrick, John C. (ed.) *The Writings of George Washington from the Original Manuscript Sources, 1745—1799,* vols. 39 Washington, DC, 1944.

Ford, Paul Leicester.(ed.) *The Writings of Thomas Jefferson.* New York: G. P. Putnam's Sons, 1892–1899.

Friedrich, Carl. *Constitutional Government and Democracy: Theory and Practice in Europe and America.* Boston: Ginn & Co., 1950.

DOI: 10.1057/9781137539625.0008

_____ "The Problem of Constitutional Dictatorship," in *Public Policy: A Yearbook of the Graduate School of Public Administration, Harvard University*, edited by C. J. Friedrich and Edward S. Mason. (Cambridge, MA: Harvard University Press, 1940).

Gattuso, John. *Washington D.C.: Know the City Like a Native*. Singapore: APA Publications, 2008.

Halstead, T. J., and Congressional Research Service. *Presidential Signing Statements: Constitutional and Institutional Implications*. Washington, DC: Congressional Research Service, Library of Congress, 2007.

Hamilton, Alexander, James Madison, and John Jay. *The Federalist Papers*. New York: Bantam Press, 1982.

Harrington, James. "The Commonwealth of Oceana," in The Commonwealth of Oceana and A System of Politics, edited by J.G.A. Pocock (Cambridge: Cambridge University Press, 1992).

Heidler, David S. and Jeanne T. Heidler. *The War of 1812*. Westport, CT: Greenwood Press, 2002.

Herodotus. "Writings on Athenian Democracy" in *Classics of Moral and Political Theory*, edited by Morgan (Hacket Publishing, Indianapolis, 2001).

Herz, Michael. "Imposing Unified Executive Branch Statutory Interpretation." *Cardozo Law Review* 15, no. 1–2 (October 1993): 219–72.

Hickey, Donald. *The War of 1812: A Forgotten Conflict*. Urbana: University of Illinois Press, 1989.

Hobbes, Thomas. "Leviathan," in Classics of Moral and Political Theory, 4th edition, edited by Morgan (Indianapolis: Hackett Publishing Co, 2005).

Howe, Daniel Walker. *What Hath God Wrought: The Transformation of America 1815–1848*. New York: Oxford University Press, 2007.

Howe, John. "Republican Thought and the Political Violence of the 1790s." *American Quarterly* 19, no. 2 (Summer 1967): 147–65.

Hunt, Gaillard. *The Life of James Madison*. New York: Russell & Russell, 1968.

Jackson, Andrew. *Narrative and Writings of Andrew Jackson, of Kentucky*. Miami, FL: Mnemosyne Publishing, 1969.

Jefferson, Thomas. *The Writings of Thomas Jefferson*, edited by Paul Leicester (Ford. New York: G. P. Putnam's Sons, 1892–899).

Kagan, Elena. "Presidential Administration." *Harvard Law Review* 114, no. 8 (June 2001): 2245–2385.

Kelley, Christopher. *Executing the Constitution: Putting the President Back into the Constitution*. Albany: State University of New York Press, 2006.

DOI: 10.1057/9781137539625.0008

Keteham, Ralph Louis. (ed.) *The Anti-Federalist Papers; And, the Constitutional Convention Debates*. New York: New American Library, 1986.

Kinkopf, Neil. "Index of Presidential Signing Statements, 2001–2007." *American Constitution Society of Law and Policy*. August 2007.

Knox, J. Wendell. *Conspiracy in American Politics, 1787–1815*. New York: Arno Press, 1972.

Kohn, Richard. *Eagle and Sword: The Federalists and the Creation of the Military Establishment in America, 1783–1802*. New York: Free Press, 1975.

——— "The Washington Administration's Decision to Crash the Whiskey Rebellion." *Journal of American History* 59, no. 3 (December 1972): 567–84.

Lawson, Gary and Guy Seidman. *The Constitution of Empire: Territorial Expansion and American Legal History*. New Haven, CT: Yale University Press, 2004.

Lincoln, Abraham. *Abraham Lincoln: Speeches and Writings, 1832–1858: Speeches, Letters, and Miscellaneous Writings, the Lincoln–Douglas Debates*, edited by Don E. Fehrenbacher. (New York: Library of America, 1989).

——— *Abraham Lincoln: Speeches and Writings, 1859–1865: Speeches, Letters, and Miscellaneous Writings, Presidential Messages and Proclamations*, edited by Don E. Fehrenbacher. (New York: Literary Classics of the United States, 1989).

Locke, John. "Second Treatise on Government," in *Classics of Moral and Political Theory*, edited by Morgan (Cambridge, New York: Cambridge University Press, 1993).

Lund, Nelson, "Guardians of the Presidency: The Office of the Counsel to the President and the Office of Legal Counsel" in *Government Lawyers: The Federal LegalBureaucracy and Presidential Politics*, edited by Cornell W. Clayton (Kansas: University Press of Kansas, 1995).

Lynch, Timothy. *Breaking the Vicious Cycle: Preserving Oar Liberties while Fighting Terrorism*. Washington, DC: CATO Institute, June 26, 2002.

Machiavelli, Niccolò, "Discourses on the First Ten Books of Titius Livius," excerpts reprinted in *Classics of Moral and Political Theory*, 3rd edition, edited by Morgan (Indianapolis: Hackett, 2001), pp. 467–87.

Madison, James. *The Papers of James Madison*. Chicago: University of Chicago Press, 1962.

——— *Writings*, edited by Jack N. Rakove. New York: Library of America, 1999.

DOI: 10.1057/9781137539625.0008

Malone, Dumas. *Jefferson the President: The First Term, 1801–1805.* Boston: Little, Brown, 1970.

_____ *Jefferson the President: The Second Term, 1805–1809.* Boston: Little, Brown, 1974.

Martin, Kate. "Legal Detainment?" Center for National Security Studies, *SAIS Review* 29, no. 1 (Winter–Spring 2004).

Matheson, Scott M. Jr. *Presidential Constitutionalism in Perilous Times.* Cambridge, MA: Harvard University Press, 2009.

May, Christopher. "Presidential Defiance of 'Unconstitutional' Laws: Reviving the Royal Prerogative." *Hastings Constitutional Legislative Quarterly* 21, no. 4 (1994): 865–1011.

Mayer, John. "Outsourcing Torture: The Secret History of America's Extraordinary Rendition Program." *New Yorker.* February 14, 2005.

McDonald, Forrest. *Presidency of George Washington.* Lawrence: University Press of Kansas, 1974.

Meacham, Jon. *American Lion: Andrew Jackson in the White House.* New York: Random House, 2008.

Meese, Edwin. *With Reagan: The Inside Story.* Washington, DC: Regnery Gateway, 1992.

Mill, John. *Representative Government.* New York: Dutton, 1950.

Montesquieu, "Spirit of the Laws," in *Classics of Moral and Political Theory* edited by Morgan (New York: Hafner Publishing Co., 1966).

Morgan, Michael. (ed.) *Classics of Moral and Political Theory.* Indianapolis, IN: Hackett Publishing Co., 1992.

Neustadt, Richard E. *Presidential Power and the Modern Presidents: The Politics of Leadership from Roosevelt to Reagan.* New York: Free Press, 1990.

Nicolay, John G., and John Hay. *Abraham Lincoln: A History.* New York: Century Co., 1890.

Paine, Thomas. *Common Sense.* Mineola, NY: Dover Thrift Editions, 1997.

Pearce, Roy Harvey. *Savagism and Civilization: A Study of the Indian and the American Mind.* Berkeley: University of California Press, 1988.

Pfiffner, James P. *Power Play: The Bush Presidency and the Constitution.* Washington, DC: Brookings Institution, 2008.

Phelps, Glenn. *George Washington and American Constitutionalism.* Lawrence: University Press of Kansas, 1993.

Pierson, William Whatley. "The Committee on the Conduct of the Civil War." *The American History Review* 23, no. 3 (April 1918): 550–76.

DOI: 10.1057/9781137539625.0008

Plato, "Republic," in *Classics of Moral and Political Theory*, edited by Morgan (Indianapolis, IN: Hackett, 2001).

Polybias, "History of Rome," in *The Oxford History of the Classical World*, edited by John Boardman, Jasper Griffin, and Oswyn Murray. (Oxford, New York: Oxford University Press, 1986).

Prakash, Saikrishna B., and Michael D. Ramsey. "The Executive Power over Foreign Affairs." *Yale Law Journal* 111, no. 2 (November 2001): 299–300.

Randall, James Garfield. *Constitutional Problems under Lincoln*. New York, London: Appleton and Co., 1926.

Remini, Robert. *Andrew Jackson and the Course of American Freedom*. Baltimore, MD: Johns Hopkins University Press, 1998.

———— *Andrew Jackson and His Indian Wars*. New York: Viking, 2001.

———— "The Constitution and the Presidencies: The Jackson Era," in *The Constitution and the American Presidency*, edited by Martin L. Fausold and Alan Shank, 34–56. (Albany: State University of New York Press, 1991).

———— *The Life of Andrew Jackson*. New York: Harper & Row, 1988.

Richardson, James Daniel. *A Compilation of the Messages and Papers of the Presidents, 1789–1897*. Washington, DC: Government Printing Office, 1896–1899.

Risen, James. *State of War: The Secret History of the CIA and the Bush Administration*. New York: Free Press, 2006.

Rossiter, Clinton. *Constitutional Dictatorship: Crisis Government in the Modem Democracies*. Princeton, NJ: Princeton University Prose, 1948.

Rousseau, Jean-Jacques, "The Social Contract," in *Classics of Moral and Political Theory* edited by Morgan (Indianapolis IN: Hackett Publishing Company, 1992).

Savage, Charlie. *Takeover: The Return of the Imperial Presidency and the Subversion of American*. New York: Little, Brown, 2007.

Schelling, Thomas. "Hamilton and Emergency Power." *Journal of Strategy and Conflict* 18 (1960): 34–36.

Schlesinger, Arthur Jr. *The Age of Jackson*. Boston: Little, Brown, 1945.

Schmitt, Gary. "Jefferson and Executive Power: Revisionism and the Revolution of 1800." *Publius* 17, no. 2 (Spring 1987): 7–25.

Slaughter, Thomas. *The Whiskey Rebellion: Frontier Epilogue to the American Revolution*. New York: Oxford Press, 1986.

DOI: 10.1057/9781137539625.0008

Smelser, Marshall. "The Jacobin Phrenzy: Federalism and the Menace of Liberty, Equality, and Fraternity." *The Review of Politics* 13, no. 4 (October 1951): 457–82.

Sofaer, Abraham. *War, Foreign Affairs and Constitutional Power: The Origins.* Cambridge, MA: Ballinger Publishing Co., 1976.

Storing, Herbert J. and Murray Dry. *The Complete Anti-Federalist.* Chicago: University of Chicago Press, 1981.

Syrett, Harold Coffin, ed. *The Papers of Alexander Hamilton.* New York: Columbia University Press, 1961.

Thach, Charles. *The Creation of the Presidency, 1775–1789: A Study in Constitutional History.* Baltimore, MD: Johns Hopkins University Press, 1922, 1969.

U.S. Department of Justice. Department of Justice Inspector General Issues Report on Treatment of Aliens Held on Immigration Charges in Connection with the investigation of the September 11 Terrorist Attacks. June 2, 2003. www.justice.gov/oig/special/0306/press.pdf.

Watkins, Frederick Mundell. *The Failure of Constitutional Emergency Powers under the German Republic.* Cambridge, MA: Harvard University Press, 1939.

Wilentz, Sean. *Andrew Jackson.* New York: Times Books, 2005.

Williams T. Harry. "The Committee on the Conduct. of the War." *The Journal of the American Military Institute* 3, no. 3 (Autumn 1939): 138–56.

Wills, Gary. *Bomb Power: The Modern Presidency and the National Security State.* New York: Penguin, 2009.

Woodward, Bob. *Bush at War.* New York: Simon and Shuster, 2002.

Yoo, Cristopher, Steven G. Calabresi, and Anthony J. Colangelo. "The Unitary Executive in the Modern Era, 1945–2004." *Iowa Law Review* 90, no. 2 (2005): 601–731.

Yoo, John C. *Crisis and Command: The History of Executive Power from George Washington to George W. Bush.* New York: Kaplan, 2009.

_____ *Memorandum Re: Authority for Use of Military Force to Combat Terrorist Activities within the United States.* October 23, 2001. U.S. Department of Justice, Office of Legal Counsel.

_____ *Memorandum Re: Constitutionality of Amending Foreign Intelligence Surveillance Act to Change the "Purpose" Standard for Searches.* September 25, 2001. U.S. Department of Justice.

DOI: 10.1057/9781137539625.0008

Index

DOI: 10.1057/9781137539625.0009

DOI: 10.1057/9781137539625.0009

DOI: 10.1057/9781137539625.0009

DOI: 10.1057/9781137539625.0009

DOI: 10.1057/9781137539625.0009

CPSIA information can be obtained at www.ICGtesting.com
Printed in the USA
LVOW11*1726230616

493846LV00008B/49/P

9 781137 539618